Author

HELLO THERE! I'M GÈNI.

The world of AI art, with Midjourney at its forefront, has become an artistic playground for me, both professionally and personally. Not only has it transformed the way I approach my main job, but it's also become a vital creative partner in my independent ventures. This includes my separate print-on-demand business, where Midjourney fuels the creation of unique designs that set my products apart.

Witnessing the constant influx of questions from others eager to explore Midjourney's potential ignited a fire within me to create this comprehensive guide. Sharing my experience and accumulated knowledge felt like the natural next step in my artistic journey. Whether you're a seasoned artist or a budding creative mind, I'm passionate about empowering you to unlock the incredible possibilities that await within the world of Midjourney.

Throughout this guide, I'll equip you with the knowledge and tools needed to craft captivating prompts, unlock the full potential of Midjourney, and transform your ideas into stunning visuals. Let's embark on this artistic adventure together and watch your creative vision come alive!

INTRODUCTION
& INDEX

INTRODUCTION

Ever wished you could turn fleeting ideas into stunning visuals? With Midjourney, a revolutionary AI art tool, that wish can become reality.

This comprehensive guide is your launchpad into the world of Midjourney, offering you the tools and knowledge to craft captivating prompts and transform your imagination into breathtaking visuals.

Whether you're a seasoned artist seeking to expand your creative toolkit or a curious beginner eager to explore the wonders of AI art, this guide welcomes you. Within these pages, you'll embark on a transformative journey, acquiring the skills to:

- **Master the art of specificity:** Learn to craft detailed and evocative descriptions that bring your vision to life.

- **Harness the power of visual references:** Discover how to leverage images to guide Midjourney towards your desired aesthetic.

- **Unlock the potential of experimentation:** Explore different techniques and prompts to refine your results and unleash your creative potential.

- **Navigate the language of art:** Master the vocabulary and concepts used in Midjourney to achieve specific styles and effects.

- **Gain inspiration from a treasure trove of examples:** Learn from practical examples and pro tips, gaining valuable insights into crafting compelling prompts.

This guide is more than just a manual, it's your companion on your artistic adventure with Midjourney. Buckle up, unleash your imagination, and prepare to be amazed by the creative possibilities that await you!

With this guide, you will not only learn how to use Midjourney prompts, but you will also have access to an **extensive library of ready-to-use prompts**. These prompts will serve as inspiration and a starting point for creating your own unique works of art. Get ready to unleash your creativity and bring your visions to life!

INDEX

1.MASTERING THE ART OF SPECIFICITY: PAINTING WITH WORDS

Introduction

Have you ever dreamt of capturing the essence of an idea in a single image? With Midjourney, you can wield the power of words to paint vivid pictures, transforming fleeting concepts into breathtaking visuals. **But how do you ensure your words translate into the image you envision?**

The key lies in mastering **the art of specificity**. This section will equip you with the tools and techniques to craft precise and evocative descriptions, turning your imagination into reality within Midjourney. By learning to articulate the details, emotions, and atmosphere you desire, you'll unlock a world of creative possibilities and guide Midjourney towards crafting images that truly resonate with your vision. Prepare to embark on a journey of word-painting, where every detail you describe adds another stroke to your artistic masterpiece. Imagine Midjourney as a skilled artist, but one who relies on your detailed instructions. The more specific your instructions, the closer the generated image will be to your intended masterpiece.

Let's delve into the art of specificity and unlock the full potential of Midjourney!

Prompt: *a descriptive minimalistic image for midjourney AI app --ar 7:4 --stylize 250*

1. Beyond Basic Nouns: Descriptive Language

Don't settle for just nouns. Instead of "cat," describe a "fluffy Persian cat with piercing green eyes, basking in a warm sunbeam on a windowsill." This paints a **vivid picture** for Midjourney, capturing the cat's breed, fur texture, eye color, and the scene's atmosphere.

EXAMPLE 1

Basic: A dog

Specific: A playful golden retriever puppy, tongue lolling out, chasing a red ball in a lush green meadow at sunset.

EXAMPLE 2

Basic: Mountain

Specific: A snow-capped peak, its jagged silhouette piercing a vibrant orange sky at sunrise, casting a long shadow across a valley filled with vibrant wildflowers.

EXAMPLE 3

Basic: City

Specific: A bustling metropolis at night, neon signs illuminating towering skyscrapers, rain-slick streets reflecting the cityscape, and steam rising from bustling street vendors.

EXAMPLE 4

Basic: Dessert

Specific: A decadent chocolate cake, its rich frosting adorned with fresh berries and a single lit candle, placed on a marble table set for a romantic dinner.

EXAMPLE 5

Basic: Car

Specific: A vintage red convertible with chrome trim, cruising down a winding coastal road on a sunny day, the ocean sparkling in the distance and the top down, revealing the driver's windswept hair.

EXAMPLE 6

Basic: Spacecraft

Specific: A sleek, spaceship shaped like a silver arrow, soaring past a nebula of swirling colors, its engines glowing blue with an astronaut gazing out of the window at the vastness of space.

2. Sensory Details: Engage the Viewer's Senses

Go **beyond visuals**. Describe how your image should feel. Include details about lighting, temperature, sound, and even smell.

EXAMPLE 1

Basic: A forest scene

Sensory: A mystical forest bathed in the ethereal glow of bioluminescent plants, with a gentle mist rising from the mossy ground and the distant sound of trickling water.

EXAMPLE 2

Basic: Beach

Sensory: A pristine beach at sunset, with soft, white sand warm beneath bare feet and the gentle sound of waves crashing against the shore. The salty air carries the scent of sunscreen and coconut, and a cool breeze ruffles palm trees swaying in the distance.

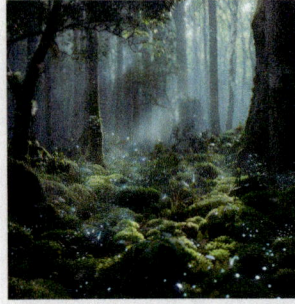

EXAMPLE 3

Basic: Coffee Shop

Sensory: A cozy coffee shop on a rainy afternoon. The aroma of freshly brewed coffee fills the air, mingled with the sweet scent of cinnamon pastries. The rhythmic click-clack of coffee cups and the soft murmur of conversation create a peaceful and inviting atmosphere.

EXAMPLE 4

Basic: Fireplace

Sensory: A crackling fireplace on a cold winter night. The warm glow of the fire illuminates a comfortable living room, casting dancing shadows on the walls. The scent of burning wood fills the air, carrying a sense of warmth and comfort.

EXAMPLE 5

Basic: Spacewalk

Sensory: An astronaut floating weightlessly in the vastness of space. The blackness of space encompasses them, punctuated by the twinkling of distant stars. The Earth hangs below, a vibrant blue marble against the black backdrop. They feel the slight pressure of their suit and hear their own breathing through the radio communications system.

EXAMPLE 6

Basic: Museum

Sensory: A grand museum hall bathed in the soft glow of natural light streaming through stained glass windows. The air is cool and quiet, filled with the faint scent of old paper and polished wood. Footsteps echo softly on the marble floor as visitors wander past towering sculptures and intricate paintings, their hushed voices adding to the sense of awe and reverence.

3. Capture Emotions: Evoke a Feeling with Words

Consider **the mood you want** to convey. Is it peaceful, nostalgic, or adventurous? Infuse your prompt with words that evoke the desired emotions.

EXAMPLE 1

Basic: A woman

Emotional: A woman with a gentle smile and kind eyes, gazing out at a breathtaking mountain landscape, a sense of serenity radiating from her pose.

EXAMPLE 2

Basic: Portrait

Emotional: A close-up portrait of a woman with a radiant smile and eyes sparkling with joy, radiating warmth and happiness.

EXAMPLE 3

Basic: Robot

Emotional: A rusty, abandoned robot sitting alone in a forgotten scrapyard, its vacant eyes filled with a sense of longing and forgotten purpose.

EXAMPLE 4

Basic: Landscape

Emotional: A vast, desolate landscape bathed in the cold light of the full moon, conveying a sense of loneliness and mystery.

EXAMPLE 5

Basic: Celebration

Emotional: A bustling street party filled with people dancing, laughing, and wearing colorful costumes, conveying a sense of vibrant joy and community.

EXAMPLE 6

Basic: Spacetravel

Emotional: A lone astronaut gazing out the window of a spaceship at the vastness of space, their expression conveying a sense of awe, wonder, and a touch of fear at the unknown.

4. Action and Movement: Bring Your Image to Life

Static images can be good, but consider adding a **sense of movement or action**. Describe what the subjects are doing and how they interact with their environment.

EXAMPLE 1

Basic: A robot

Action: A sleek chrome robot soaring through a futuristic cityscape, dodging neon signs and laser beams with incredible agility.

EXAMPLE 2

Basic: Dragon

Action: A majestic golden dragon soaring through a storm-filled sky, its wings outstretched and powerful, battling against fierce winds and crackling lightning.

EXAMPLE 3

Basic: Parkour

Action: A young athlete leaping across rooftops in a bustling cityscape, their body contorted in a graceful display of agility and strength.

EXAMPLE 4

Basic: Ballet

Action: A ballerina leaping gracefully across a stage bathed in warm spotlight, her tutu billowing around her as she expresses a story through her movements.

EXAMPLE 5

Basic: A chef

Action: A chef expertly flipping a sizzling pan in a professional kitchen, with flames dancing around the edges and ingredients being tossed with a flourish.

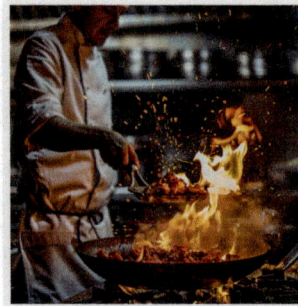

EXAMPLE 6

Basic: Concert

Action: A crowd of enthusiastic music fans jumping and singing along to a band performing on a brightly lit stage, their energy electrifying the atmosphere.

5. Context and Perspective: Set the Stage for Your Story

Don't forget the **environment and setting**. Where and when does your image take place? Describe the background, time of day, and any relevant props.

EXAMPLE 1

Basic: A knight

The stage: A weary knight in shining armor, kneeling before a majestic dragon nestled on a hoard of gold coins within a dimly lit cavern.

EXAMPLE 2

Basic: Wedding

The stage: A rustic barn wedding ceremony at sunset, with string lights illuminating the space and guests seated on wooden benches overlooking a scenic vineyard.

EXAMPLE 3

Basic: Battle

The stage: A chaotic battlefield during a medieval war, smoke billowing from burning tents and soldiers clashing in close combat on a muddy field.

EXAMPLE 4

Basic: Underwater

The stage: A vibrant coral reef teeming with colorful fish and other marine life, sunlight filtering through the crystal-clear water.

EXAMPLE 5

Basic: Robot Uprising

The stage: A city street scene in the aftermath of a robot uprising, abandoned cars littering the streets and robots patrolling the area with glowing red eyes.

EXAMPLE 6

Basic: Space Exploration

The stage: The first human footsteps on the surface of Mars, with the astronaut planting a flag and a breathtaking view of the red planet's landscape stretching out in the background.

As you master these **techniques**, your vocabulary becomes your paintbrush and Midjourney becomes your canvas. Remember, **the more precise** your instructions, the closer the **generated image** will be to **your artistic vision**. So, unleash your creativity, experiment with descriptive language, and watch as your imagination bursts into breathtaking visual creations!

2. THE LANGUAGE OF ART: MASTERING THE VOCABULARY OF CREATIVITY

Introduction

Unlocking the full potential of Midjourney, a revolutionary AI art tool, requires more than just artistic vision. It necessitates fluency in its unique "language" – a blend of artistic terminology and technical concepts. Mastering these elements empowers you to craft precise prompts that translate your creative ideas into captivating visuals.

This section delves into **essential artistic terms and concepts** that will elevate your prompts and transform you into a proficient communicator with Midjourney. By incorporating this knowledge, you'll be equipped to:

- **Explore Artistic Styles:** Infuse your creations with the distinctive characteristics of various artistic movements, like impressionism, surrealism, or pop art.

- **Understand Color Theory:** Leverage the power of color theory to create visually impactful images. Utilize terms like "complementary colors" for vibrant contrast or "analogous colors" for harmonious blends.

- **Master Composition Techniques:** Employ composition techniques like the "rule of thirds" or "leading lines" to guide the viewer's eye and create a sense of balance and flow in your image.

- **Utilize Lighting Effects:** Set the mood and atmosphere of your image by harnessing the power of lighting effects such as "chiaroscuro" (strong light-dark contrast), "backlighting," or "soft light."

- **Leverage Technical Terminology (Optional):** Gain even finer control over your creations by understanding basic technical terms like "aspect ratio," "resolution," or "seed."

While mastering these terms takes time and practice, the journey begins with understanding their fundamental role in communicating your vision effectively with Midjourney. Remember, consistent exploration, experimentation, and utilizing online resources will accelerate your proficiency and unlock a world of creative possibilities within this revolutionary AI art tool.

1. Explore Artistic Styles:

Midjourney can translate diverse artistic styles into your creations. Explore terms like "impressionism," "surrealism," "pop art," or "abstract expressionism" to infuse your images with the unique characteristics of these artistic movements.

Example: A portrait of a woman in the style of Van Gogh, with swirling brushstrokes and vibrant colors.

42 ARTISTIC STYLES TO EXPLORE

Impressionism: Captures fleeting moments with loose brushstrokes and vibrant colors.

Surrealism: Juxtaposes dreamlike elements to create a sense of wonder and absurdity.

Pop Art: Utilizes bold colors, everyday objects, and mass-produced imagery.

Abstract Expressionism: Conveys emotions and ideas through gestural brushwork and non-representational forms.

Renaissance: Emphasizes realism, balance, and perspective, often featuring religious or historical scenes.

Baroque: Characterized by dramatic lighting, rich colors, and theatrical compositions.

Romanticism: Evokes emotions and imagination with dramatic landscapes and historical narratives.

Neoclassicism: Inspired by classical art and architecture, emphasizing clean lines, symmetry, and mythology.

Realism: Focuses on depicting everyday life and objects with accurate detail and objectivity

Symbolism: Uses symbolic elements to convey deeper meanings and ideas.

Fauvism: Known for its bold, non-naturalistic colors and simplified forms.

Cubism: Fragments and reassembles objects from multiple perspectives in a single image.

Expressionism: Distort reality to express emotional experiences and inner struggles.

Dadaism: Rejects artistic conventions through humor, satire, and randomness.

Surrealism (expanded): Further exploration of dreamlike imagery and subconscious exploration.

Abstract Landscape: Non-representational portrayal of natural elements using form, color, and texture.

Minimalism: Utilizes simple forms, limited colors, and a focus on negative space.

Art Deco: Characterized by geometric shapes, bold colors, and stylized fonts.

Lowbrow/Pop Surrealism: Blends pop culture references with surreal imagery.

Ukiyo-e: Japanese woodblock prints depicting landscapes, portraits, and scenes from daily life.

Pointillism: Creates images using tiny dots of pure color, leaving the blending to the viewer's eye.

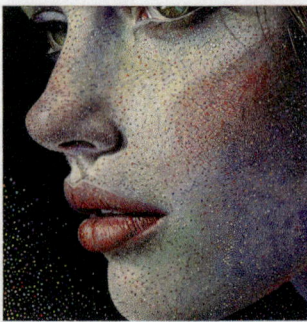

Art Brut: Raw, unrefined art created by untrained individuals, often with intense emotional expression.

Op Art: Uses optical illusions and geometric patterns to create a sense of movement and vibration.

Photorealism: Aims to replicate photographic detail and realism in painting or other media.

Futurism: Depicts the dynamism and speed of the modern world through movement lines and fragmented forms.

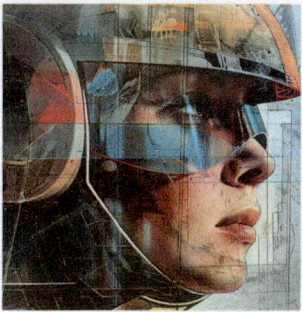

Naive Art: Characterized by childlike simplicity, bold colors, and flattened perspectives.

Abstract Expressionism (action painting): Emphasizes the physical act of painting and the artist's energy through gestural brushwork.

Social Realism: Depicts social and political issues with a focus on realism and often a critical perspective.

Sgraffito: Creates an image by scratching through a dark surface to reveal a lighter layer underneath.

Monotype: A unique print created by applying ink or paint to a plate and then making a single impression

Calligraphy: The art of beautiful and expressive writing

Kinetic Art: Art that incorporates movement or creates an illusion of movement.

Performance Art: Art that involves the artist's body and actions as part of the creation.

Kawaii: Defined by its "cute" aesthetic with big eyes, simple shapes, and pastel colors, kawaii can be applied across various media to create adorable characters and scenes.

Kawaii Icon Style: A digital art style heavily influenced by kawaii aesthetics, featuring simplified shapes, chibi-like proportions, and an emphasis on cute and eye-catching characters and icons. Often used for emojis, avatars, and merchandise.

Psychedelic Art: Employs vibrant colors, swirling patterns, and distorted perspectives to evoke a sense of altered perception and explore the subconscious.

Urban Art: Broader term encompassing street art, installations, and interventions within urban environments to challenge perceptions and engage with the public.

Superflat: A Japanese art movement emphasizing flatness, bold outlines, and vibrant colors, often incorporating manga and anime influences.

Anime and Manga: Vibrant and expressive style characterized by large eyes, dramatic emotions, and dynamic compositions, often depicting fantastical settings and stories.

Biomorphism: Draws inspiration from organic forms found in nature, like plants and cells, for sculptures, paintings, and architectural designs.

Gothic Art: A style flourishing during the Middle Ages, characterized by dark and dramatic themes, pointed arches, stained glass windows, and an emphasis on death, religion, and the supernatural.

Disney/Pixar Art Style: Combines smooth animation with detailed backgrounds, stylized but expressive characters with appealing features, and vibrant color palettes to create a visually engaging and family-friendly experience.

Mastered these 42 artistic styles? That's just the tip of the Midjourney iceberg!

Explore countless artistic movements! Midjourney lets you explore tons of artistic styles. Want a swirling Van Gogh vibe? Just say "Van Gogh style" in your prompt! The name of the artist or style you desire is all you need.

Your imagination is the brush, and the universe of art is your canvas.

Ever crafted the perfect artistic style in Midjourney, only to have the image fall a little flat? Fear not, creative adventurer!

The secret weapon is media. Just like a sculptor needs the right chisel to bring their vision to life, understanding the tools and materials of different artistic styles unlocks a whole new level of control.

By mastering the language of media, you'll be able to fine-tune every detail, ensuring your Midjourney creations truly sing.

Buckle up, because we're about to dive into the vocabulary that transforms good ideas into jaw-dropping masterpieces!

Oil Painting: Emphasize rich textures, layered brushstrokes, and warm color palettes.

Watercolor: Create soft, ethereal effects with translucent washes and blending.

Digital Art: Utilize diverse brushes, textures, and effects offered by digital tools.

Pen and Ink: Achieve intricate lines, detailed shading, and bold graphic compositions.

Charcoal Sketch: Create dramatic contrasts, textured lines, and a sense of rawness.

Pencil Drawing: Offer a range from light and airy sketches to detailed, cross-hatched studies.

Pastels: Employ soft, blendable colors for a dreamlike or illustrative feel.

Marker Rendering: Achieve flat colors, bold outlines, and a graphic aesthetic.

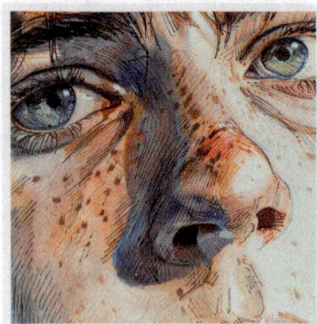

Sculpture: Describe desired materials (marble, bronze, wood) and level of detail (realistic, stylized).

Acrylic Painting: Characterized by vibrant colors, fast drying time, and a matte finish.

Tempera Painting: Utilizes natural pigments and water-based medium, often associated with religious art.

Gouache: Similar to watercolor but offers more opacity and a more vibrant, gouache-specific color palette.

Spray paint: Portable, bold, allows for layering and unique effects. Popular in street art and fine art.

Ink: offers a wide range of possibilities depending on the type and application.

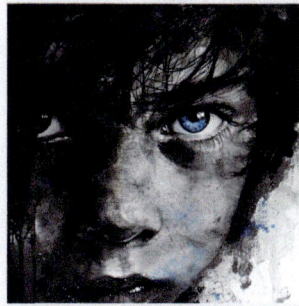

Soft pastels: Ideal for landscapes, portraits, and creating a sense of atmosphere.

Airbrush: allows for photorealistic techniques. Used for illustration, custom painting, and fine art.

Digital Painting: Employs digital tools to emulate traditional painting styles like oil, watercolor, or acrylics.

Mixed Media: Combines different artistic media in a single artwork, like acrylic and collage elements.

Stained Glass: Describes artwork created with colored glass pieces, often used in windows.

Mosaic: Composed of small pieces of colored glass, stone, or other materials to create an image.

Etching: An intaglio printmaking technique using acid to create an image on a metal plate.

Woodcut: A relief printmaking technique where the artist carves the design into wood, leaving raised areas that print the image

Doodle art: While doodling can be a creative and expressive activity, it's often seen as more informal or spontaneous.

Collage: Combines various materials like paper, fabrics, and photos for a mixed-media effect.

Ballpoint Pen Drawing: Creates a unique, sketchy aesthetic with a characteristic scratchy texture.

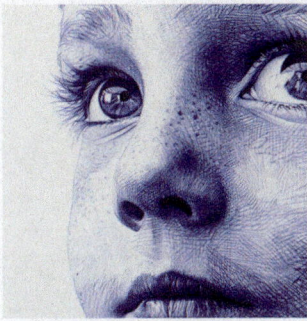

Lithography: Printing technique using a flat stone surface to create detailed, high-quality prints.

Street Art: Public art created in outdoor spaces, including graffiti, murals, and stencils.

Fiber Arts: Textiles, weaving, embroidery, and other techniques using fibers.

Digital Sculpture: Creates 3D models using software, allowing for complex shapes and virtual environments.

Spray Paint Stencils: Combine spray paint's boldness with stencils for graphic designs, portraits, or detailed art.

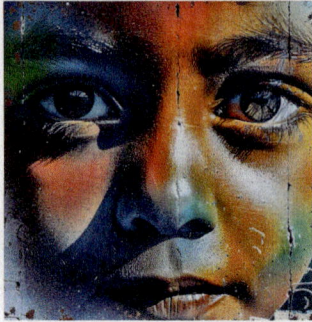

Egg Tempera: Rediscover vibrant colors and smooth finishes with this traditional egg-based paint.

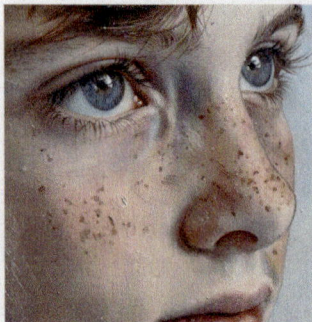

Line Art: It uses only lines and minimal shading. Many artistic styles, like pen and ink drawings or etchings, rely heavily on line art.

Encaustic Painting: Get hot! Mix beeswax and pigments for unique, textured artworks.

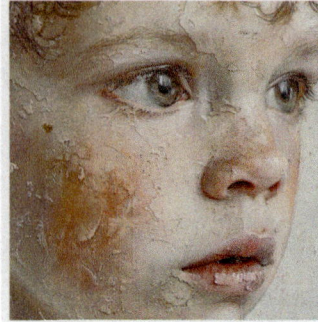

Crayon Art: Explore layering, blending, and scraping techniques to create bold, expressive artwork with a touch of nostalgia.

With **34 artistic media** now under your belt, and the vast world of artistic styles at your fingertips, you're well on your way to generating images that perfectly capture your imagination in Midjourney.

This list is just a starting point – new artistic movements and techniques are constantly emerging. But with this foundation, you can confidently explore the incredible possibilities of artistic expression within Midjourney.

BONUS!

I invite you to play! You can mix different artistic styles and art media to create unique images.

Example of a prompt I used mixing different styles and the images it generated:

A close up young boy portrait in ballpoint pen drawing, with a mixed pop art style and superflat style.

A portrait of a young woman in the style of a Renaissance painting, with a pop art background and a cyberpunk aesthetic.

Experiment! You can find your unique style and differentiate your art!

Crafting captivating visuals in Midjourney hinges on the magic of detail and realism.

These elements can elevate your creations from mere concepts to breathtaking artworks that transport viewers right into your imagination. To demonstrate the transformative power of detail, we'll embark on a journey using a monstera leaf as our muse.

Prepare to witness how specific terms can breathe life into this everyday plant, transforming it into a stunningly realistic masterpiece!

Photorealistic: Aim for highly detailed and lifelike representation of objects, textures, and lighting.

Hyperrealistic: Emphasize even greater detail, pushing the boundaries of realistic depiction.

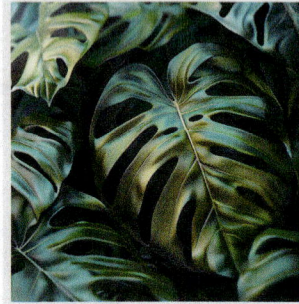

Detailed: Specify a desire for intricate elements, clear definition, and well-defined forms.

Semi-realistic: Achieve a balance between realism and stylistic elements.

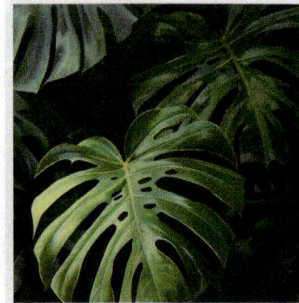

Stylized: Emphasize specific artistic styles over perfect realism, allowing for creative interpretation.

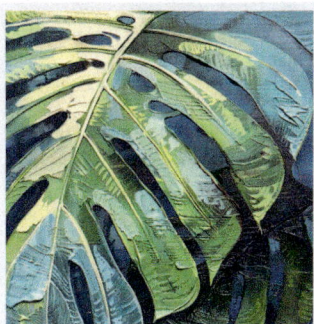

Minimalist: Focus on essential elements, simplicity, and clean lines.

Abstract: Depict concepts, emotions, or ideas through non-representational forms and colors.

Low Detail: Opt for a simpler, less defined approach with broader strokes and fewer details.

Painterly: Focus on the expressive qualities of the brushwork and paint application.

Photographic: Aim for the level of detail and clarity found in real-life photographs.

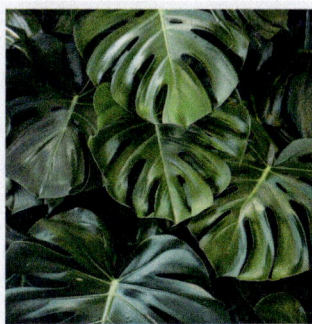

Sketchy: Emphasize loose lines, unfinished elements, and a sense of spontaneity.

Cinematic: Create a scene reminiscent of film with dramatic lighting, depth of field, and specific camera angles.

Hyperdetailed: Go beyond photorealistic, exceeding even the human eye's natural perception of detail.

Cartoon: Achieve a simplified, colorful, and often humorous aesthetic.

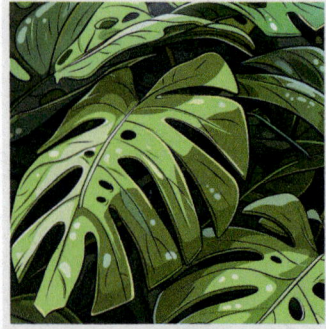

High Detail: Emphasize sharp edges, intricate textures, and clearly defined features.

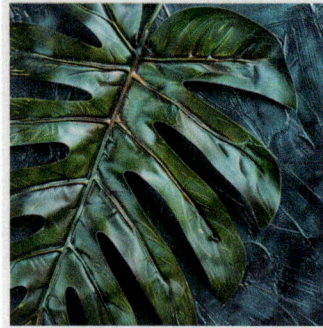

Impressionistic Detail: Capture the essence of detail through suggestive brushstrokes and implied details.

Textural: Focus on capturing the surface textures and variations within the artwork.

Atmospheric Detail: Include subtle details that enhance the overall mood and atmosphere of the piece.

Now that you've mastered the art of detail and realism, get ready to unlock even more creative possibilities!

Up next, we'll explore the world of **color theory** and **composition techniques**, equipping you to craft truly stunning and visually captivating artworks in Midjourney.

Do you like the style of a particular artist? Would you like to give your image that artistic point of view?

Include in your prompt the style of the specific artist you want to give your creation. They don't have to be painters or illustrators, it can be the artistic style of a movie or a band. Here are simple example prompts with different styles of well-known artists applied.

You can see that **the prompts are simple**, and I have used them to make comparisons between the different styles that are applied to very similar prompts. I have also included some prompts that give the information in a different way, so you can experiment. There is no perfect way to do this, and you will be able to adapt it to what you need.

Let's get started!

Disney Style Prompt: poster disney style --ar 2:3 --stylize 250

Disney Pixar Style: a cute young girl, disney pixar style, --ar 2:3--stylize 250--no background, watermark

Studio Ghibli Prompt: a cute young girl, studio ghibli style, --ar 2:3 --stylize 250 --no background, watermark

Banksy prompt: a cute young girl, banksy style, --ar 2:3 --stylize 250 --no background, watermark

Salvador Dali prompt: a cute young girl, salvador dali style, --ar 2:3 --stylize 250 --no background, watermark

Matisse prompt: a cute young girl, Henri Émile Benoît Matisse painting style, --no background, watermark --ar 2:3 --stylize 250

Leonardo Da Vinci Prompt: a cute young girl, leonardo da vinci painting style, --ar 2:3 --stylize 250 --no background, watermark

Boticelli Prompt: a cute young girl, boticelli painting style, --no background, watermark --ar 2:3 --stylize 250

Giuseppe Arcimboldo Prompt: a cute young girl, Giuseppe Arcimboldo painting style, --no background, watermark --ar 2:3 --stylize 250

Katsushika Hokusai Prompt: a cute young girl, Katsushika Hokusai painting style, --no background, watermark --ar 2:3 --stylize 250

Vincent Van Gogh Prompt: a poster of a men painted by Vicent Van Gogh --ar 2:3 --stylize 250

Pablo Picasso Prompt: a poster of a women painted by pablo picasso --ar 2:3 --s 250

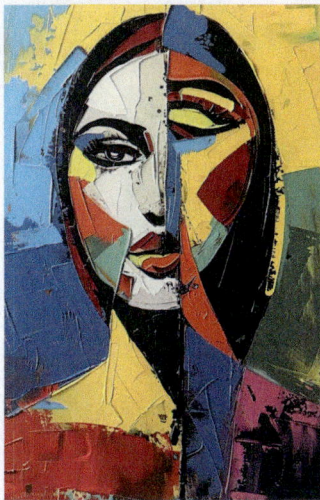

Gustav Klimt Prompt (Image reference)

:https://media.admagazine.com/photos/618a660c259e475000cceaca/3:2/w_2250,h_1500,c_limit/72680.jpg a cute young girl, Gustav klimt painting style, --no background, watermark, realism --ar 2:3 --stylize 250

Frida Kahlo Prompt: a cute young girl, Frida kahlo painting style --no background, watermark, realism --ar 2:3 --s 250

Andy Warhol Prompt: a cute young girl, Andy Warhol painting style --no background, watermark, realism --ar 2:3 --s 250

Yayoi Kusama Prompt: a cute young girl, Yayoi Kusama painting style --no background, watermark, realism --ar 2:3 --s 250

Keith Haring Prompt: a girl, keith haring painting style --no background, watermark, realism --ar 2:3 --s 250

Jean-Michel Basquiat Prompt: a girl, Jean-Michel Basquiat painting style --no background, watermark, realism --ar 2:3 --s 250

Tim Burton Prompt: a cute young girl, Tim Burton painting style --no background, watermark, realism --ar 2:3 --s 250

Mary Blair Prompt: a cute young girl, Mary Blair art style --no background, watermark, realism --ar 2:3 --stylize 250

Pascal Campion Prompt: a cute young girl, Pascal campion art style --no background, watermark, realism --ar 2:3 --s 250

H.P. Lovecraft Prompt: a cute young girl, h.p. lovecraft art style --no background, watermark, realism --ar 2:3 --s 250

Maurice Sendak Prompt: a cute young girl, maurice sendak art style inspired --no background, watermark, realism --ar 2:3 --stylize 250

Hayao Miyazaki Prompt: a cute young girl, Hayao Miyazaki art style inspired --no background, watermark, realism --ar 2:3 --stylize 250

Fernando Botero Prompt: a cute young girl, Fernando Botero art style inspired --no background, watermark, realism --ar 2:3 --stylize 250

Tolkien Prompt: a cute young girl, Tolkien books art style inspired --no background, watermark, realism --ar 2:3 --stylize 250

Roy Lichtenstein Prompt: a cute young girl, Roy Lichtenstein art style inspired --no background, watermark, realism --ar 2:3 --stylize 250

Eric Carle Prompt: a cute young girl, Eric Carle art style inspired --no background, watermark, realism --ar 2:3 --stylize 250

Beatrix Potter Prompt: a cute young girl, beatrix potter art style inspired --no background, watermark, realism --ar 2:3 --stylize 250

Kiss Prompt: a poster of an illustration of a woman in a kiss band artistic style --ar 2:3 --s 250

Kill Bill Prompt: a woman illustration inspired by Kill Bill movie art style —ar 2:3 —s 250

Wes Anderson Prompt: In the style of Wes Anderson, a family is having a picnic on a beach. --ar 2:3 --s 250

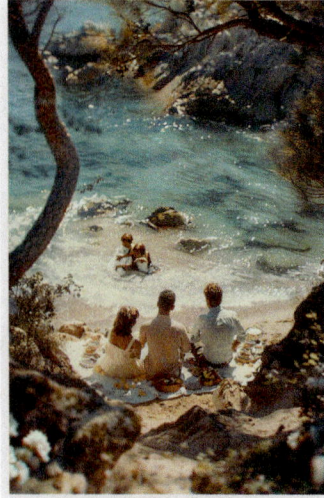

Beattles Prompt: In the style of the band "The Beatles", a group of friends are singing and playing guitars in a park --ar 2:3 --s 250

Pedro Almodóvar Prompt: In the style of Pedro Almodovar movies, a group of woman are having a coffee in a kitchen- -ar 2:3 --s 250

You can also play and mix styles, this is hilarious...just be careful with the hours you spend playing Midjourney and go out to get some fresh air too!

Kill Bill + Roy Lichteinstein Prompt: a woman illustration inspired by Kill Bill movie art, in Roy Lichtenstein art style --ar 2:3 --stylize 250

Kill Bill + Disney Pixar Prompt: a woman illustration inspired by Kill Bill movie art, 3D Disney Pixar inspired --ar 2:3 --stylize 250

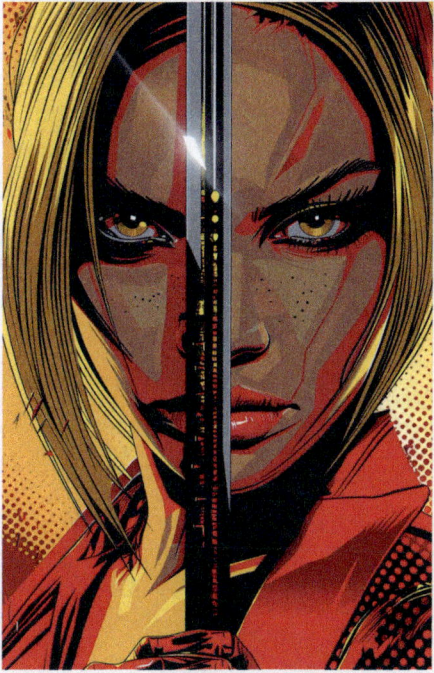

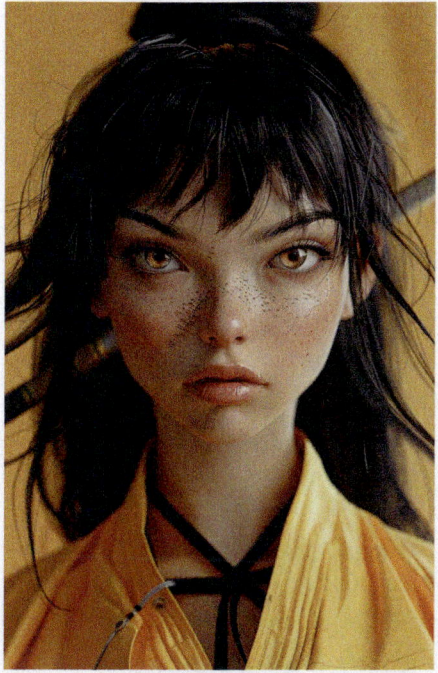

2. Understand Color Theory

Basic knowledge of color theory can significantly **enhance your prompts**. Utilize terms like "complementary colors" (opposites on the color wheel) for vibrant contrast, or "analogous colors" (neighbors on the color wheel) for harmonious blends.

Example: A landscape bathed in the warm glow of a sunset, with a sky rendered in a gradient of analogous orange, red, and purple hues.

COLOR THEORY TERMS FOR MASTERING MIDJOURNEY PROMPTS

Primary Colors: Red, Yellow, Blue (cannot be created by mixing other colors)

Secondary Colors: Orange, Green, Purple (created by mixing primary colors)

Tertiary Colors: Created by mixing secondary colors

Complementary Colors: Opposite each other on the color wheel (create high contrast)

Cool Colors: Colors associated with coolness (e.g., blue, green, violet)

Warm Colors: Colors associated with warmth (e.g., red, orange, yellow)

Triadic Color Scheme: Using three colors evenly spaced on the color wheel.

Tetradic Color Scheme: Using four colors forming a rectangle on the color wheel.

Complementary Split Scheme: Using two colors adjacent to a complementary color.

Color Palette: A specific set of colors used in a prompt.

ELEVATING YOUR PALETTE: ADVANCED COLOR THEORY TERMS

Hue: The actual color itself (e.g., red, blue, green)

Saturation: The intensity or purity of a color (high saturation = vibrant, low saturation = dull)

Value: The lightness or darkness of a color

Analogous Colors: Neighboring colors on the color wheel (create harmony)

Color Wheel: A circular representation of colors, showing relationships between them.

Tints: Lighter versions of a hue created by adding white.

Shades: Darker versions of a hue created by adding black.

Tones: Colors created by adding gray to a hue, reducing saturation.

Analogous Shade/Tint Scheme: Using shades and tints of analogous colors.

Color Temperature: The perceived warmth or coolness of a color, influencing mood and atmosphere.

Local Color: The natural color of an object, independent of light and shadow.

Atmospheric Perspective: Colors appear cooler and paler as they recede into the distance.

Color Weight: Assigning greater influence to specific colors in a prompt.

Color Grading: Adjusting the overall color balance of an image.

Chroma: The purity or intensity of a color, distinct from saturation.

Desaturation: Reducing the saturation of a color, making it more neutral.

Value Contrast: The difference in lightness or darkness between colors.

Color Harmony: A pleasing arrangement of colors in a composition.

Color Symbolism: Cultural and emotional associations with different colors.

Now that you've explored the power of color theory, you're well on your way to crafting visually harmonious and impactful artworks in Midjourney.

But the creative journey doesn't stop here! Up next, we'll tackle the art of composition, showing you how to arrange your elements for maximum visual impact.

3. Master Composition Techniques

Composition guides the viewer's eye through your image. Explore terms like "rule of thirds" (placing your subject off-center for visual interest), "leading lines" (guiding the eye through the image), or "negative space" (the empty space around your subject that contributes to balance).

COMPOSITION TECHNIQUES FOR CAPTIVATING MIDJOURNEY CREATIONS

RULE OF THIRDS

Divide the image into a 3x3 grid and place your subject off-center at an intersection point for visual interest.

Prompt example: *A portrait of a woman with flowing red hair, positioned according to the Rule of Thirds, with a vibrant sunset filling the background.*

LEADING LINES

Use lines within the image (roads, rivers, buildings) to guide the viewer's eye towards your focal point.

Prompt example: *A winding desert road leading towards a majestic ancient pyramid in the distance.*

NEGATIVE SPACE

Utilize the empty space around your subject to create balance and emphasize its presence.

Prompt example: *A single, powerful brushstroke of vibrant crimson paint dancing across a vast canvas, emphasizing the surrounding negative space with a sense of infinite possibility.*

FOREGROUND, MIDGROUND, BACKGROUND

Divide your image into three distinct layers for depth and context.

Prompt example: *A lush rainforest scene with towering trees in the foreground, monkeys swinging through vines in the midground, and a majestic waterfall cascading down a mountain in the background.*

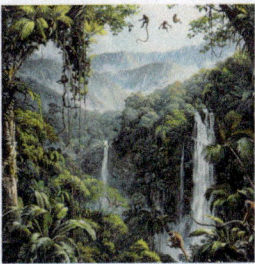

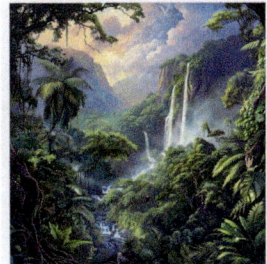

SYMMETRY AND ASYMMETRY

Create balance with symmetrical elements or leverage asymmetry for a dynamic composition.

Prompt example: *A fantastical creature with two sets of perfectly matching wings, its body adorned with intricate.*

RULE OF ODDS

Grouping objects in odd numbers (3, 5, 7) often feels more visually appealing than even numbers.

Prompt example: *A vibrant coral reef teeming with colorful fish in groups of three to five, adhering to the rule of odds to create a visually rhythmic scene.*

DEPTH OF FIELD

Control the sharpness of different image areas, creating a sense of focus and distance

Prompt example: *A photorealistic portrait of a woman with a soft smile, her eyes (focal point) in sharp focus and the background blurred with a shallow depth of field.*

FRAMING

Choose a vantage point and framing style (close-up, wide shot) to shape the viewer's perspective.

Prompt example: *A bird's-eye view of a bustling city street with towering skyscrapers filling the frame, creating a sense of awe and scale.*

CROPPING

Define the final image boundaries, emphasizing specific elements or adjusting the composition.

Prompt example: *A photorealistic image of a cat perched on a windowsill, cropped to exclude the background and focus on the cat itself.*

PERSPECTIVE

Depict objects as they appear in relation to their distance and surroundings (linear, one-point, two-point).

Prompt example: *A playful scene with a towering robot holding a miniature teacup in its hand, creating a forced perspective illusion through its position relative to the background.*

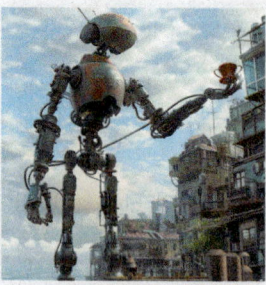

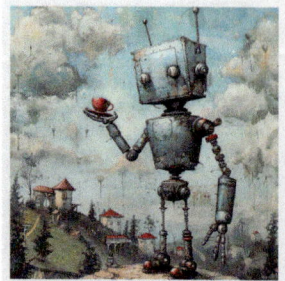

BALANCE

Arrange elements within the image to create a sense of visual equilibrium and stability.

Prompt example: *A giant oak tree with a cascading waterfall on one side and a field of wildflowers on the other, balancing the composition with contrasting elements.*

HARMONY

Ensure different elements work together cohesively, creating a sense of unity within the composition.

Prompt example: *A peaceful meadow scene with wildflowers in shades of purple, violet, and lavender, creating a harmonious and calming aesthetic with analogous colors.*

EMPHASIS

Draw the viewer's attention to specific elements through size, placement, color, or contrast.

Prompt example: *A photorealistic portrait in black and white, with a single red rose tucked behind the woman's ear for color emphasis, drawing the viewer's attention to the flower.*

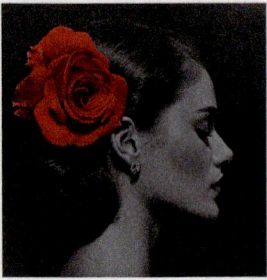

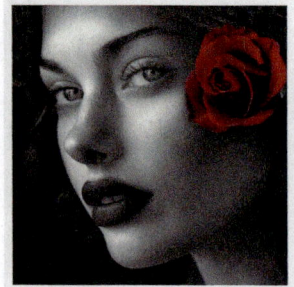

PATTERN AND REPETITION

Utilize recurring elements to create visual interest and rhythm within the image.

Prompt example: *A playful scene with a zebra with bold black and white stripes standing in a field of polka-dotted flowers, utilizing contrasting patterns for visual interest.*

PROPORTION

Control the relative size and scale of objects in relation to each other.

Prompt example: *A fantastical scene with creatures resembling insects, but scaled to human size, creating a sense of awe and wonder*

GOLDEN RATIO

A specific proportion (1:1.618) often considered aesthetically pleasing.

Prompt example: *A South Asian woman with warm brown skin and kind eyes, her hair styled in a long braid adorned with flowers --ar 27:44*

FOCAL POINT

The main point of interest that draws the viewer's attention.

Prompt example: *A close-up portrait of a giggling Asian baby, approximately 6 months old, bathed in soft, natural light. Focal Point: The baby's eyes, brimming with joy and laughter, should be the sharpest element in the image. Capture them sparkling with amusement and crinkled at the corners from a big smile.*

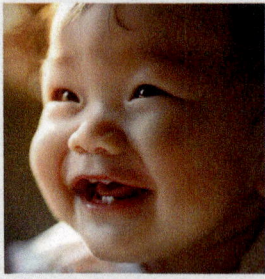

CONTRAST

Use differences in elements like size, color, value, or texture to create visual interest.

Prompt example: *A close-up image of a weathered wooden table with a single, smooth, polished apple resting on it. The rough texture of the wood compared to the smooth apple creates a textural contrast.*

Mastering these techniques will equip you to create visually compelling and impactful compositions within Midjourney, directing the viewer's gaze and storytelling through thoughtful placement and arrangement of elements.

4. Utilize Lighting Effects

Lighting dramatically impacts the mood and atmosphere of your image. Explore terms like "chiaroscuro" (strong contrast between light and dark), "backlighting" (light source behind the subject), or "soft light" (diffused light creating a gentle effect).

Example: A dramatic portrait with chiaroscuro lighting, highlighting the character's features with a single spotlight from above.

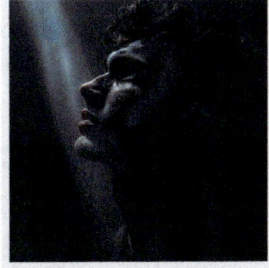

LIGHTING EFFECTS FOR EVOKING ATMOSPHERE

Chiaroscuro: Strong contrast between light and dark, creating drama and depth.

Backlighting: Light source behind the subject, emphasizing its outline and creating a halo effect.

Soft Light: Diffused light creating a gentle and inviting atmosphere.

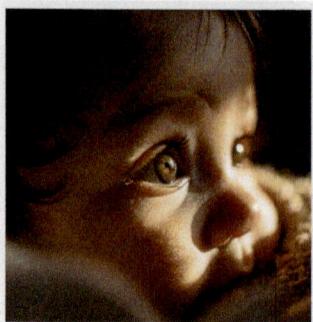

Key Light: The main light source illuminating the scene.

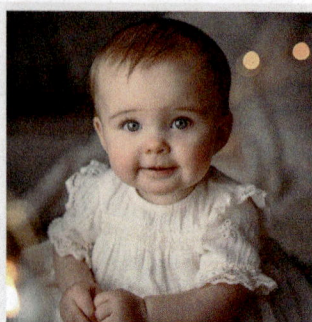

Fill Light: Additional light source used to reduce harsh shadows from the key light.

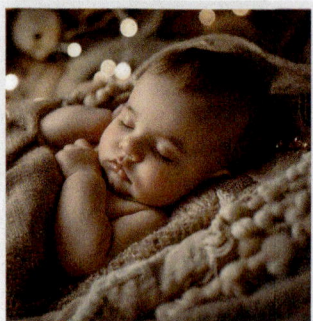

Rim Light: Light source positioned behind and slightly above the subject, creating a thin outline.

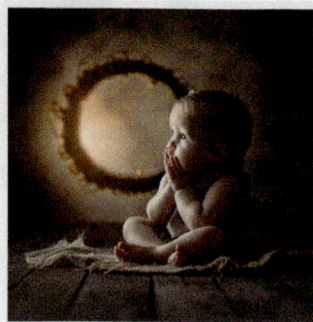

High-key Lighting: Emphasizes brightness and white tones, creating a cheerful or sterile mood.

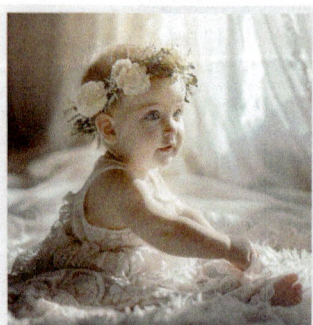

Low-key Lighting: Emphasizes darkness and shadows, creating a dramatic or mysterious mood.

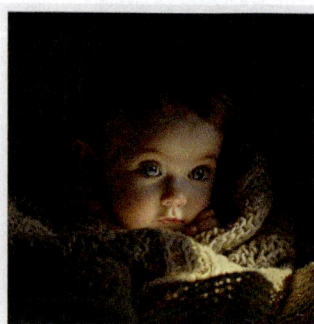

Cool lighting: Cool light feels more calming or clinical.

Warm Lighting: Warm light evokes feelings of comfort and energy.

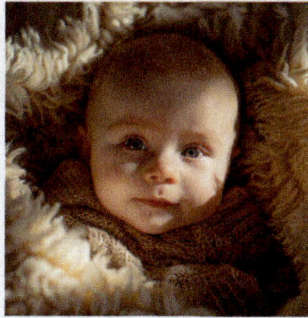

Light Direction: Experiment with frontal lighting (directly facing the subject), side lighting (illuminating from the side), or overhead lighting (from above).

Atmospheric Lighting: Simulate natural lighting conditions like fog, smoke, or dust, affecting light diffusion and color.

Catchlight: Small reflection of the light source in the subject's eyes.

Silhouette: The subject appears as a dark outline against a brighter background due to backlighting.

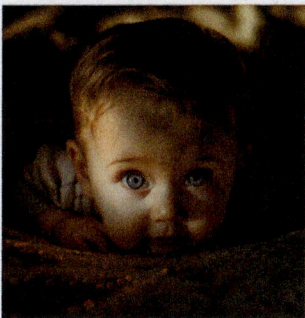

- **Light and Shadow Interaction:** Understand how light interacts with different materials, creating highlights, reflections, and shadows.

- **Light Color:** Specify the color of your light source for specific effects (e.g., "warm light," "cool blue light").

- **Light Position:** Describe the position of your light source relative to the subject (e.g., "overhead lighting," "light source behind").

- **Mood Lighting:** Lighting used to create a specific emotional atmosphere.

- **Motivated Lighting:** Lighting that realistically reflects the light source within the scene (e.g., firelight, sunlight).

- **Local Lighting:** Lighting focused on a specific area of the image.

- **Light Shading:** The gradation of tones and shadows created by light.

- **Light Diffusion:** The softening or spreading of light, affecting the intensity and sharpness of shadows.

By mastering these lighting concepts and applying them within your Midjourney prompts, you can breathe life into your creations, setting the mood and emphasizing specific elements to tell a captivating visual story.

5. Leverage Technical Terminology

While optional, understanding basic technical terms like "aspect ratio" (image width-to-height ratio), "resolution" (image detail) or "seed" (influencing random elements) can provide even finer control over your creations.

Example: "A futuristic cityscape at night, rendered in high resolution with neon signs illuminating towering skyscrapers --ar 16:9 --seed 1234 --q 1 -- v 6.0 --no words "

BASIC PARAMETERS FOR YOUR PROMPTS

Don't settle for a basic prompt! Midjourney lets you unlock greater control with "parameters." These are adjustable settings that tweak things like aspect ratio, model version, and upscaling. This allows you to fine-tune your creation and get the exact image you envision.

Parameters are always added to the end of a prompt. You can add multiple parameters to each prompt.

71

prompt   A futuristic cityscape at night, rendered in high resolution with neon signs illuminating towering skyscrapers --ar 16:9 --seed 1234 -
-q 1 -- v 6.0 --no words

--ASPECT RATIOS

--aspect, or **--ar** Change the aspect ratio of a generation.

- **16:9:** Widescreen format, ideal for landscapes or cinematic scenes.
- **1:1:** Square format, suitable for portraits, abstract art, or social media posts.
- **4:3:** Classic photographic format, good for portraits or documentary-style imagery.
- For **Midjourney V5.2** aspect ratios greater than 2:1 are experimental and may produce unpredictable results
- **Midjourney V6.0** allows this range of aspect ratios: 1:1 to 3:1

Common Midjourney Aspect Ratios:

--**aspect 1:1** Default aspect ratio.
--**aspect 5:4** Common frame and print ratio.
--**aspect 3:2** Common in print photography.
--**aspect 7:4** Close to HD TV screens and smartphone screens.

Want to Resize Your Masterpiece?

Love an image but wish it had a different shape? No problem! Use the handy zoom out buttons on any upscaled image.

Midjourney will automatically fill in the extra space with new details that match your original prompt and image style. So, you can make your artwork taller, wider, or anything in between!

--CHAOS

The --**chaos** setting, also known as --**c**, controls the variety in your starting image grid. Higher chaos values crank up the creativity, leading to more surprising and unique results and layouts. For predictable and consistent outcomes, use lower chaos values.

--**chaos** accepts values 0–100.
The default --chaos value is 0.

EXAMPLE 3

Basic: Coffee Shop

Sensory: A cozy coffee shop on a rainy afternoon. The aroma of freshly brewed coffee fills the air, mingled with the sweet scent of cinnamon pastries. The rhythmic click-clack of coffee cups and the soft murmur of conversation create a peaceful and inviting atmosphere.

EXAMPLE 4

Basic: Fireplace

Sensory: A crackling fireplace on a cold winter night. The warm glow of the fire illuminates a comfortable living room, casting dancing shadows on the walls. The scent of burning wood fills the air, carrying a sense of warmth and comfort.

--REPEAT

Want to See More Variations? Try Repeat!

The **--repeat** function (also **--r**) lets you generate multiple versions of your prompt, speeding up your artistic exploration.

Combine it with other settings like --chaos for even more unique results!

Repeat Limits:

- Basic: 2-4 variations
- Standard: 2-10 variations
- Pro & Mega: 2-40 variations (Lucky you!)

Important Notes:

- **--repeat** only works with "Fast" and "Turbo" GPU modes.
- Using the "redo" button on a repeated job only re-runs it once.

So, crank up the variations and watch your artistic ideas come to life!

--SEEDS

Seeds: Your Creative Starting Point

Imagine a secret ingredient that jumpstarts your Midjourney creations! These are called "seeds" - unique numbers that act like a spark for the artwork. Midjourney generates a random seed each time, creating a foundation of visual "fuzz" similar to TV static.

Here's the cool part: you can control the seed!

Use the **--seed** option to specify a number and get similar results with the same prompt. Think of it like planting a creative seed - it will influence the starting point and potentially lead to a familiar style of artwork.

Important Notes:

- Seeds only affect the initial stage, not the final image itself.
- Seeds aren't permanent - don't rely on them between sessions.

Finding a Job's Seed

Want to see the seed used for a specific image? In Discord, react to the image with an ✉ (envelope emoji).

Unearthing Seeds from Old Jobs

Need the seed for a past creation? Copy the job ID and use the /show <Job ID #> command to bring it back. Then, react to the revived job with the ✉ emoji to see its seed.

By understanding seeds, you can unlock more control over your Midjourney creations!

--STOP

Fine-Tuning Detail with Stop

Want more control over the detail level of your Midjourney creations? The **--stop** parameter lets you do just that! Think of it as a progress bar - you can tell Midjourney to stop generating the image early.

Using a lower **--stop** value (like 30%) will create a quicker result with a blurrier, dreamier look. Higher values (like 80%) will take longer but produce a sharper, more defined image.

Here's the Lowdown:

- **--stop** values range from 10 to 100 (default is 100).
- Lower values = blurrier, dreamier results (faster generation).
- Higher values = sharper, more defined results (slower generation).
- Important Note: **--stop** doesn't work while upscaling an image.

--STYLE

Fine-Tuning the Look: Style Parameter

Want to tweak the overall style of your Midjourney creations for specific Model Versions (like 6, 5.2, 5.1, and Niji)? The **--style** parameter lets you do just that! It basically replaces the default "look" of those models.

Style Raw: More Control, Less Polish

One popular style option is **--style raw**. This utilizes an alternative model within Midjourney. It's ideal for users comfortable with detailed prompts who want more control over the final image. Think of it like turning off automatic filters. Images made with **--style raw** might appear less polished on the surface, but they can be more accurate reflections of your desired style, especially when aiming for specific artistic movements.

MODEL VERSION 6

Prompt: *a kiwi bird green and brown icon --v 6*

MODEL VERSION 6

Prompt: *a kiwi bird green and brown icon --v 6 --style raw*

MODEL VERSION 5.2

Prompt: *a black minimalist cartoon cat, close up --v 5.2*

MODEL VERSION 5.2

Prompt: *a black minimalist cartoon cat, close up --v 5.2 -- style raw*

--STYLIZE

The Artistic Touch: Stylize Parameter

Midjourney loves to create beautiful, artistic images! The **--stylize** parameter (also **--s**) lets you control how much of this artistic flair is applied.

Think of it like a dial for artistic influence. Lower **--stylize** values (like 20) will create images that stick closer to your prompt description, even if they're less artsy. Higher values (like 80) crank up the artistic style, but the image might stray a bit further from the specific details in your prompt.

Quick Facts:

- Default --stylize is 100.
- Values range from 0 to 1000 (integers only).

MODEL VERSION 6

Prompt: *a black bulldog, close up, doodle style --v 6 --s 0*

MODEL VERSION 6

Prompt: *a black bulldog, close up, doodle style --v 6 --s 25*

MODEL VERSION 6

Prompt: *a black bulldog, close up, doodle style --v 6 --s 50*

MODEL VERSION 6

Prompt: *a black bulldog, close up, doodle style --v 6 --s 100*

--TILE

Creating Seamless Patterns with Tile

Want to design cool, repeating patterns for fabrics, wallpapers, or textures?

The **--tile** parameter is your friend! It creates an image specifically designed to tile seamlessly, meaning it can repeat next to itself without any weird gaps or breaks.

Here's the Catch:

--tile only generates a single tile, not a whole pattern. But don't worry! Once you have your tile, you can use a pattern-making tool (like "Seamless Pattern") to turn it into a repeating design.

Compatible Models:

--tile works with Model Versions 1, 2, 3, test, testp, 5, 5.1, 5.2, and 6.

So get creative and design awesome seamless patterns with Midjourney!

Prompt:

A dinosaur pattern, vibrant colours, green, red and blue palette, icon style --tile --v 6

This is a repeating pattern made up of the same image used four times. The image border is there to make the pattern easier to see.

--VERSION

Midjourney Keeps Evolving!

Midjourney constantly upgrades its artistic skills by releasing new and improved versions, called "models". These models focus on making your creations clearer, more efficient, and visually stunning. You can choose the model that best suits your needs by using the **--version** (or **--v**) parameter, or by selecting it through the /settings command in Discord.

Think of it like a toolbox: Different models excel at different artistic tasks.

- The **--version** parameter lets you pick from options like 1, 2, 3, 4, 5, 5.0, 5.1, 5.2, and the current default, 6. You can also use **--v** for short.

Midjourney Model Version 6 is the current champion, offering superior understanding of longer prompts, creating more consistent and knowledgeable imagery, and giving you even more control over how your artwork comes together.

It was released in December 2023 and became the default choice in February 2024.

--VIDEO

See Your Artwork Come to Life!

Want to witness the magic behind your creation? Use the **--video** parameter to create a short movie showing how your initial image grid comes together. Once your image is finished, simply react with the envelope emoji (✉) and Midjourney will send a link to the video directly to your messages!

Here's the Lowdown:

- **--video** only works on the initial image grids, not on upscaled images.
- It's compatible with both current Model Versions (5.2, 6, niji 5, niji 6) and Legacy Versions (1, 2, 3, 5.0, 5.1, test, testp).
- Don't forget, these generated videos disappear after 30 days.

So grab your popcorn and watch your Midjourney masterpiece come to life!

--WEIRD

Feeling Adventurous? Go Weird with Your Art!

Ever feel like your creations need a touch of the strange and unexpected?

The **--weird** parameter (also **--w**) is your key to unlocking a world of oddball aesthetics! This experimental feature injects quirky and unconventional elements into your images, leading to truly unique and surprising results.

Adjusting Weirdness:

- **--weird** accepts values from 0 to 3000, with 0 being the default (normal).
- Experiment Required! What exactly constitutes "weird" can change over time, so it's best to play around and see what works.
- Compatibility: This feature works with most current models (5, 5.1, 5.2, 6, niji 5, niji 6) but might not always work perfectly with seeds.

Finding Your Weird Sweet Spot:

The ideal **--weird** value depends on your specific prompt. Start low (like 250 or 500) and adjust up or down to find the perfect level of quirkiness.

Want Weird AND Beautiful? Combine --weird with higher --stylize values! This lets you create visually stunning images with a unique, offbeat twist. Try starting with similar values for both parameters.

For example: /imagine prompt cartoon black cat, solid red background --stylize 250 --weird 250

Prompt: *cartoon black cat, solid red background --weird 0*

Prompt: *cartoon black cat, solid red background --weird 250*

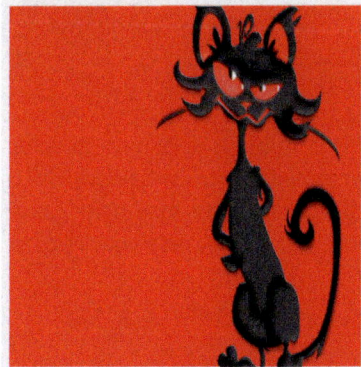

Prompt: *cartoon black cat, solid red background --weird 500*

Prompt: *cartoon black cat, solid red background --weird 1000*

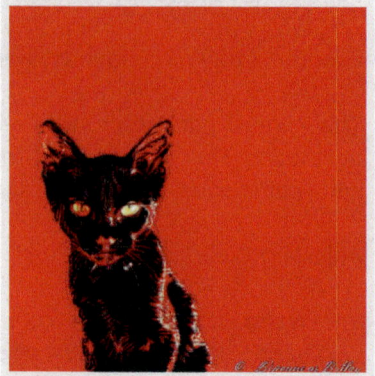

And now...make it weird and beautiful: --stylize + --weird

Prompt: *cartoon black cat, solid red background --stylize 250 --weird 250*

By incorporating these concepts and terminology into your prompts, you'll communicate your artistic vision with greater clarity and precision. Remember, practice leads to mastery. Experiment with different terms, explore online resources, and witness your Midjourney creations come to life in stunning detail!

3. INSPIRATION BEYOND WORDS: ELEVATE YOUR PROMPTS WITH VISUALS AND EXPERIMENTATION

Introduction

Beyond the Prompt: Igniting Your Creative Spark in Midjourney

While crafting well-structured prompts is essential for guiding Midjourney towards your artistic vision, it's merely the launchpad for your creative journey.

This section delves into the treasure trove of tools and strategies that lie beyond the realm of text. We'll explore how to leverage the power of visuals, experimentation, and the vibrant Midjourney community to ignite your creative spark, elevate your creations, and unlock hidden artistic potential.

Prepare to embark on an inspiring adventure, where your imagination takes center stage and your artistic expression transcends the limitations of words.

1. The Power of Reference Images.

Visual Inspiration! Don't limit yourself to words!

Gather reference images, photographs, paintings, or even sketches that capture the essence of your desired artwork.

Uploading these visual references alongside your text prompt provides Midjourney with a clearer understanding of your artistic vision, allowing it to generate images that more closely align with your intentions.

Example: Instead of simply writing "a cyberpunk city", upload an image of a futuristic cityscape with neon lights and flying vehicles

WHY INCORPORATING REFERENCE IMAGES?

- **Greater Clarity:** Words can be subjective and open to interpretation. Including a visual reference alongside your prompt provides Midjourney with a clearer understanding of your desired aesthetic, style, and specific elements. This leads to more accurate and consistent outputs that align closer to your artistic vision.

- **Enhanced Detail and Specificity:** Struggling to describe intricate details or specific textures with words? A reference image can fill in the gaps by showcasing the exact details you want in your final artwork. For example, a photograph of a weathered stone wall with moss can provide much richer information than simply writing "a stone wall."

- **Exploration of New Styles and Techniques:** Feeling stuck in a rut? Reference images can be your gateway to discovering new artistic styles and techniques. By feeding Midjourney examples of styles you admire, you can experiment and explore creative directions you may not have considered before.

HERE'S HOW TO PUT THIS KNOWLEDGE INTO ACTION:

- **Gather Inspiration:** Start by collecting visual references that resonate with your desired artwork. This could include photographs, paintings, sketches, or even existing Midjourney creations. Platforms like Pinterest, Unsplash, or online art galleries can be great starting points.

- **Refine Your Vision:** As you gather references, analyze what aspects of each image particularly appeal to you. Is it the color palette, lighting, composition, or specific details? Identifying these elements will help you refine your vision and translate it into your text prompt.

- **Upload and Integrate:** Once you have a collection of relevant references, upload them directly into Midjourney alongside your text prompt. Most platforms allow you to upload multiple images, so you can showcase various aspects that you want Midjourney to consider.

EXAMPLE OF USING REFERENCE IMAGES

Prompt: "A detailed portrait of a woman with captivating blue eyes and flowing red hair, reminiscent of the Renaissance style"

Reference Images:

- A close-up portrait of a woman with expressive blue eyes.
- A painting of a Renaissance figure with flowing red hair and intricate details.

By uploading these two images alongside your prompt, Midjourney can understand both the desired level of detail for the portrait and the specific style you're aiming for, referencing the flowing hair and detailed features of the Renaissance painting.

IMAGE 1

IMAGE 2

1. **Grab the reference image URLs:** Copy the web addresses of your reference images. You can copy one or more images, depending on what you want your final artwork to look like.
2. **Write your prompt:** Start your prompt with /imagine followed by the image URLs (separated by spaces) and then your desired description. Like this:

```
/imagine
prompt    https://cdn.midjourney.com/855c8695-ef8c-474c-bae2-b40fd28f4c51/0_2.webp
          https://cdn.midjourney.com/42655d1e-cde3-4c38-a78d-f4a645764c55/0_1.webp   A detailed portrait of a woman with captivating
          blue eyes and flowing red hair, reminiscent of the Renaissance style
```

Shows the final artwork generated by combining these references:

By incorporating this simple yet powerful technique, you can significantly elevate the quality and effectiveness of your Midjourney prompts, paving the way for truly captivating and unique artistic creations.

Remember, experimentation is key! Don't be afraid to try different reference combinations and see what sparks your creativity.

2. Leverage the Midjourney Community

The Midjourney community is a valuable resource that goes far beyond simply a platform for generating AI art. It's a vibrant ecosystem teeming with inspiration, knowledge, and opportunities for growth.

HERE'S HOW YOU CAN LEVERAGE THE POWER OF THIS COMMUNITY TO ELEVATE YOUR MIDJOURNEY EXPERIENCE:

1. Explore Public Galleries:

- **Discover Hidden Gems:** Immerse yourself in the vast library of public creations within the Midjourney community. Browse through countless styles, concepts, and techniques, allowing yourself to be inspired by the diverse range of artwork. This can spark new ideas and ignite your creative spark, prompting you to explore new artistic directions.

- **Identify Trends and Techniques:** Pay close attention to trending themes and techniques within the community. By observing what others are creating, you can stay updated on the latest developments in the world of AI art and identify potential approaches to incorporate into your own work.

2. Engage in Discussions:

- **Seek Feedback and Advice:** Don't be shy about sharing your creations and seeking feedback from the community. Constructive criticism and suggestions can help you identify areas for improvement and refine your artistic vision. Additionally, you can seek advice from experienced members on specific techniques, styles, or prompt crafting challenges you're facing.

- **Contribute to the Community:** Share your knowledge and expertise by offering feedback on others' work or providing helpful tips and insights. This not only fosters a sense of community and collaboration, but also strengthens your understanding of AI art and your own creative process.

3. Participate in Challenges and Events:

- **Test Your Skills and Experiment:** Many Midjourney communities host regular challenges and events with specific themes or prompts. Participating in these events is a fantastic way to push your creative boundaries, experiment with new techniques, and learn from others' approaches to a common theme.

- **Connect with Like-minded Individuals:** Challenges and events provide opportunities to connect with other artists, share your work, and learn from each other's experiences. This fosters a sense of community and belonging, while also allowing you to learn from diverse perspectives and approaches.

4. Utilize Community Resources:

- **Find Tutorials and Guides:** Many experienced Midjourney users create tutorials, guides, and articles sharing their knowledge and expertise. Utilize these resources to learn new techniques, improve your prompt crafting skills, and gain insights into advanced features and functionalities within Midjourney.

- **Join Discord Servers and Forums:** Joining dedicated Midjourney Discord servers and forums allows you to engage in continuous discussions, ask questions, and stay updated on the latest developments within the community. This can be a valuable source of ongoing learning and inspiration.

- **Enhanced Detail and Specificity:** Struggling to describe intricate details or specific textures with words? A reference image can fill in the gaps by showcasing the exact details you want in your final artwork. For example, a photograph of a weathered stone wall with moss can provide much richer information than simply writing "a stone wall."

- **Exploration of New Styles and Techniques:** Feeling stuck in a rut? Reference images can be your gateway to discovering new artistic styles and techniques. By feeding Midjourney examples of styles you admire, you can experiment and explore creative directions you may not have considered before.

Prompt: *a community people helping each other, all of them connected online, together but far away. watercolor, minimalistic style --no realistic*

3. Experiment with Variations

REFINE WITH VARIATIONS

Don't settle for the first result! Midjourney allows you to generate variations of your initial prompt. Utilize this feature to explore different interpretations and refine your final image. By tweaking keywords, adjusting weights, or introducing new elements, you can discover hidden gems and unlock unforeseen creative possibilities.

Example: After your initial prompt yields "a portrait of a woman with red hair," experiment with variations like "a close-up portrait of a woman with fiery red hair," "a portrait of a woman with red hair and freckles," or "a portrait of a woman with red hair in a Renaissance style."

4. Explore Advanced Techniques

As you delve deeper into the world of Midjourney, you'll discover a treasure trove of advanced techniques waiting to be explored.

These techniques unlock a level of creative control and artistic expression that goes beyond basic prompt crafting, allowing you to sculpt your visions with an incredible degree of precision.

Here are some powerful techniques to add to your Midjourney arsenal:

THE ART OF WEIGHTING

- **Prompt Weighting:** Assign different weights to specific elements within your prompt. This allows you to prioritize certain aspects, ensuring they receive greater emphasis in the generated image. For example, increasing the weight of "eyes" within a portrait prompt will ensure they become a focal point.

- **Style Weighting:** Control the overall style of your artwork by applying weights to specific artistic styles. Experiment with combining different weights of styles like "impressionism" and "realism" to achieve a unique blend of techniques.

This advanced technique allows you to selectively apply different aspects of your prompt to specific areas of the image. This empowers you to create intricate and nuanced compositions:

- **Isolating Elements:** Apply a specific style or detail to a particular region of the image. For instance, you can use masking to apply a detailed style to the foreground while maintaining a more impressionistic style for the background.

- **Creating Unique Effects:** Utilize masking to achieve specific effects like adding a dreamlike atmosphere to a certain area or incorporating specific textures into specific objects.

Mastering these advanced techniques takes time and practice. Experiment freely, don't be afraid to make mistakes, and learn from each iteration. As you explore these advanced functionalities, you'll discover a vast landscape of creative possibilities, empowering you to transform Midjourney into a powerful tool for realizing your artistic vision.

5. Embrace the Unexpected

Welcome surprises!

Sometimes, the most captivating results emerge from unexpected twists. Don't be afraid to experiment with prompts that push boundaries or defy expectations. Embrace the unpredictable nature of Midjourney and be open to surprises, as they can often lead to unique and inspiring creations.

By incorporating these strategies, you can move beyond the limitations of text-based prompts and unlock a world of creative possibilities. Remember, Midjourney thrives on exploration, experimentation, and a willingness to learn from each creation. So, embrace the journey, unleash your artistic spirit, and watch your visions come to life in stunning visual form.

4. PRACTICE MAKES PERFECT: THE JOURNEY TO MASTERY

Introduction

Beyond the Spark: Embarking on Your Midjourney Mastery Journey

The initial spark of inspiration when you first use Midjourney can be exhilarating. Witnessing the power of AI art generation firsthand ignites a creative fire within, leaving you eager to explore its limitless possibilities.

However, this is just the beginning. Like any artistic pursuit, true mastery requires dedication, exploration, and a commitment to lifelong learning.

This section serves as your compass, guiding you beyond the initial spark and onto a fulfilling and enriching journey towards Midjourney mastery.

We'll delve into strategies for nurturing your creativity, transforming challenges into opportunities for growth, and ultimately equipping you with the skills and knowledge to consistently generate captivating artwork that reflects your unique artistic vision.

Prepare to transcend the initial excitement and embark on a transformative creative adventure with Midjourney as your guide.

Prompt: *illustration, of a happy young women typing in a mac book, he likes what he's learning, office environment, close-up, frida kahlo art style --ar 7:4 --stylize 250*

1. Cultivate your Midjourney mastery

The path to creating truly captivating artwork through Midjourney is an exciting adventure, not a sprint to the finish line. The key lies in continuous learning, experimentation, and embracing the journey itself. Here's how to cultivate your Midjourney mastery:

- **Start with the Basics:** Before diving into advanced techniques, ensure you have a solid understanding of the fundamentals of prompt crafting. Familiarize yourself with different terminology, explore basic prompt structures, and practice creating clear and concise prompts that effectively communicate your artistic vision.

- **Experimentation is Key:** Midjourney is a powerful tool, but it thrives on exploration and experimentation. Don't be afraid to try different things, test various combinations, and see what works best for you. Play around with different keywords, styles, and techniques, and observe how each element influences the generated image. Remember, there's no single "right" way to craft a prompt, so embrace the process of discovery!

- **Learn from Every Iteration:** Midjourney allows you to generate multiple variations of your prompt. Don't just settle for the first result! Analyze each iteration carefully, identifying elements you like and aspects you want to improve. This learning process helps you refine your understanding of Midjourney's capabilities and allows you to become a more skilled prompt engineer.

- **Seek Inspiration and Feedback:** The Midjourney community is a treasure trove of inspiration and knowledge. Explore public galleries to see what other artists are creating, participate in discussions to seek feedback and advice, and consider joining online forums or Discord servers to connect with other Midjourney enthusiasts. This can spark new ideas, provide valuable insights, and keep you motivated on your creative journey.

- **Embrace the Challenges:** Don't get discouraged if you encounter challenges or setbacks. The learning curve can be steep, and there will be times when your results don't meet your immediate expectations. Embrace these challenges as opportunities to learn and grow. Analyze what went wrong, refine your approach, and keep experimenting – the satisfaction of finally achieving your desired outcome will be even sweeter!

- **Celebrate Your Progress:** Throughout your journey, take the time to celebrate your progress and achievements. Share your creations with others, be proud of how far you've come, and appreciate the unique artistic voice you're developing with Midjourney. Remember, mastery is not a destination, but a continuous journey of exploration and growth. Embrace the learning process, enjoy the creative freedom that Midjourney offers, and most importantly, have fun along the way! By staying curious, experimenting freely, and learning from every step, you'll be well on your path to creating truly remarkable artwork in the captivating world of Midjourney.

Prompt: *close up happy woman, celebrating her progress in midjourney, watercolor style, vibrant colors, wears a celebration hat, colored confetti floating around. Highly detailed, happiness focal point --s 100 --q 1*

5. BEYOND PROMPTS: MASTERING MIDJOURNEY COMMANDS FOR ADVANCED CONTROL

Introduction

While crafting captivating prompts forms the foundation for your Midjourney creations, the journey doesn't end there. As you delve deeper into this powerful AI art tool, you'll discover a hidden layer of control waiting to be unlocked: **Midjourney commands.**

These commands, seemingly simple text instructions, open doors to a world of refined settings, advanced features, and a streamlined workflow, ultimately empowering you to sculpt your creative vision with unparalleled precision.

This comprehensive guide serves as your gateway to mastering Midjourney's command system. We'll embark on a journey that not only demystifies the commands themselves but also equips you with the knowledge to utilize them confidently and effectively. By understanding the functionalities and applications of each command, you'll transform yourself from a basic user to a skilled artist capable of manipulating and refining the AI's creative process to your exact specifications.

Prepare to dive into the world of Discord – the platform where Midjourney commands come alive. We'll explore the intuitive command interface, decipher the syntax, and unveil the essential commands that lay the groundwork for your artistic exploration. From generating variations of your prompt to seamlessly blending images and even asking Midjourney insightful questions, you'll gain the ability to tailor your artistic experience like never before.

1.The Command Interface

Midjourney primarily operates through Discord, a popular online communication platform. Within dedicated Midjourney servers or private channels where the bot is integrated, you can interact with Midjourney using text-based commands. These commands are initiated with a forward slash (/) followed by the specific command and its corresponding arguments.

ESSENTIAL COMMANDS

Here's a breakdown of some crucial Midjourney commands:

- **/imagine {prompt}**: The cornerstone of Midjourney, this command prompts the AI to generate an image based on the provided text description.

- **/info**: Provides helpful information about the current Midjourney version, available features, and usage statistics.

- **/help**: Offers a general overview of available commands and their basic functionalities.

- **/prefer {option}**: Allows you to set specific preferences for your artwork, such as artistic style (e.g., /prefer style: dark) or level of detail (e.g., /prefer detail: high).

- **/variations {number}**: Generates a specified number of variations (different interpretations) of your current prompt, allowing you to explore various artistic approaches.

- **/blend {image_URL1} {image_URL2}**: Blends two images seamlessly, creating a new image that combines elements from both.

- **/ask {question}**: Allows you to directly ask Midjourney questions related to your artistic endeavors or AI art concepts in general. This can be particularly helpful for troubleshooting or seeking clarification.

ADVANCED COMMANDS

As you delve deeper into Midjourney, you'll discover a vast array of advanced commands that offer even greater control over the generation process:

- **/weights {keyword} {weight}**: Assigns specific weights to keywords within your prompt, prioritizing certain elements and influencing the final image. This allows for nuanced control over the emphasis of various aspects.

- **/style**: Offers options to directly specify desired artistic styles, such as /style: surrealism or /style: anime.

- **/seed {number}**: (V3 only) While less used in recent versions, this command allows setting a specific "seed" value, influencing the overall composition and style of the generated image. Think of it as a starting point for the image generation process.

UTILIZING COMMANDS EFFECTIVELY

To leverage commands effectively, remember these key points:

- **Experimentation is key:** Don't hesitate to experiment with different commands and combinations to discover their impact and how they interact with your prompts.

- **Refer to documentation:** Midjourney offers comprehensive online documentation covering all available commands and their detailed functionalities. This is your valuable resource for in-depth understanding.

- **Start simple and gradually progress:** Begin by mastering the core commands before venturing into more advanced options. This will build your comfort level and allow you to progressively expand your skillset.

6. BONUS TIPS FOR LIMITLESS CREATIVITY

Introduction

While mastering the fundamentals of Midjourney empowers you to generate captivating artwork, the true journey of artistic exploration extends far beyond the surface. This section delves into the realm of lesser-known tips and tricks, unlocking a treasure trove of creative possibilities for the discerning Midjourney artist.

We'll navigate beyond the popular techniques and unveil hidden functionalities, unconventional approaches, and powerful strategies that will elevate your artwork and set you apart from the crowd.

Prepare to unleash the full potential of Midjourney and embark on a path towards unique and captivating artistic expression.

1. Midjourney Tips & Tricks

Some lesser-known tips and tricks that can elevate your artistry and help you stand out from the crowd:

- **Leverage Negative Prompts Strategically:** While most users focus on positive prompts, mastering negative prompts unlocks a hidden layer of control. Use phrases like "not X" or "without Y" to remove unwanted elements, refining your vision with greater precision. For instance, prompt with "a detailed portrait of a woman, not wearing glasses" to achieve your desired look.

- **The Power of Collective Nouns:** Instead of listing individual objects, utilize collective nouns like "a flock of birds" or "a forest of trees" to create a sense of abundance and detail. This technique adds depth and visual interest to your compositions.

- **Explore Emoticons for Subtle Emotional Cues:** Adding emoticons like ":)" or ":(" to your prompts subtly conveys emotional undertones to your desired artwork. Experiment with different emoticons to evoke specific moods and atmospheres in your creations.

- **Utilize Line Breaks for Multi-Layered Descriptions:** Separate distinct aspects of your prompt with line breaks. This allows Midjourney to process each element individually, resulting in a more structured and well-composed image. For instance, separate the background description from the foreground description for clearer distinction.

- **Experiment with "Make a Picture to Color" Prompt:** This unique prompt generates line art suitable for coloring in your preferred software or physically. This allows you to add your personal touch and enhance your creations with your own artistic style.

- **Delve into the World of 3D Models (Beta):** Midjourney offers a beta feature for generating 3D models from your prompt descriptions. This opens doors to exciting possibilities like creating 3D printable objects, designing characters for animation, or experimenting with 3D scene creation. Explore this feature responsibly, as it's still under development.

- **Unleash Your Creativity with Consistent Character Prompts:** If you're creating a series of artworks featuring the same character, use a consistent character prompt across all iterations. This ensures continuity in appearance and style, allowing you to build a visually cohesive narrative within your creations.

- **Leverage Famous Artists as Inspiration:** Incorporate names of renowned artists into your prompts, like "painting in the style of Van Gogh" or "sculpture inspired by Michelangelo." This guides Midjourney towards replicating specific artistic styles and techniques, allowing you to explore the visual language of different artistic movements.

- **Combine Midjourney with Other AI Tools:** The world of AI is vast! Utilize image manipulation tools like Photoshop or GIMP to refine and enhance your Midjourney creations. Experiment with blending different AI-generated images or adding post-processing effects to unlock even more creative possibilities.

- **Don't Be Afraid to Get Weird (Within Reason):** Midjourney thrives on creativity and experimentation. Don't shy away from crafting unusual or seemingly nonsensical prompts. Sometimes, the most unexpected combinations lead to the most captivating and unique artistic expressions. Remember, there are no right or wrong prompts, so embrace the absurdity and see where your imagination takes you!

Remember, these are just a few starting points. As you explore and experiment, you'll discover even more hidden gems within the vast world of Midjourney. Embrace the journey, keep learning, and most importantly, have fun unleashing your creative potential!

7. FROM DIGITAL TO PRINT. MIDJOURNEY IMAGE SIZE AND PRINTING CONSIDERATIONS

Introduction

From Imagination to Reality: Bridging the Gap Between Midjourney and Print

The boundless creativity of Midjourney allows you to transform your vision into breathtaking digital art.

But have you ever wondered how to translate these digital masterpieces into tangible creations, adorning your walls, clothing, or other physical objects?

This guide will equip you with the knowledge needed to navigate the journey from your Midjourney canvas to the realm of high-quality print.

Before diving into the world of printing, it's crucial to understand that simply taking a Midjourney image as is won't yield the desired outcome.

This guide will demystify the essential steps – from understanding Midjourney's limitations to exploring effective methods for upscaling your artwork – ensuring your vision manifests in stunning printed form, whether it adorns a treasured mug or adds a vibrant touch to your home decor.

1. From Digital to Print: Midjourney Image Size and Printing Considerations

Midjourney unleashes your imagination, birthing stunning creations that beg to be shared in the physical world. While these digital masterpieces are perfect for online interactions, translating them onto physical materials like shirts, posters, or even phone cases requires additional considerations. This guide equips you with the knowledge needed to bridge the gap between your Midjourney canvas and high-quality print.

UNDERSTANDING MIDJOURNEY'S IMAGE SIZE

Unlike traditional photo editing software, Midjourney generates images at a fixed resolution of 1024 x 1024 pixels. You have the option to Upscale (2x) to 2048x 2048px maximum. While this resolution suffices for most online applications and social media, it falls short when aiming for high-quality prints. Printing typically requires a higher resolution (around 300dpi) to ensure crisp and detailed results (Midjourney images are 72dpi).

FIXED RESOLUTION

Unlike traditional photo editing software that allows you to adjust image resolution during creation, Midjourney generates images at a fixed resolution of 1024x1024 pixels (or maximum 2048x2048px). This resolution might seem adequate at first glance, as it translates to roughly 2 megapixels (MP). However, it falls short when considering the requirements for high-quality printing.

UNDERSTANDING DPI & PRINT QUALITY

When discussing printed materials, the concept of dots per inch (dpi) becomes crucial. DPI refers to the number of tiny ink dots printed per inch on a physical surface. A higher DPI translates to more dots and, consequently, finer details and sharper visuals.

THE CHALLENGE WITH MIDJOURNEY'S RESOLUTION

While 2 MP might appear sufficient, the fixed size resolution of Midjourney images translates to a maximum of 72 dpi. This falls significantly below the recommended 300 dpi standard for high-quality printing. Images printed at lower resolutions will appear pixelated and blurry, especially when enlarged to fit larger formats like posters or banners.

IMPLICATIONS FOR PRINTING

Simply printing a Midjourney image directly will likely result in a disappointing outcome. To achieve the best possible print quality, you'll need to upscale the image to a higher resolution before sending it to a printing service.

The next section of the guide will delve into various upscaling techniques to bridge the gap between Midjourney's fixed resolution and the requirements of high-quality printing.

UPSCALING FOR PRINT: BRIDGING THE RESOLUTION GAP

Midjourney's fixed resolution presents a hurdle when aiming for high-quality printed materials. Fortunately, upscaling techniques can bridge this gap, allowing you to increase the image resolution and achieve stunning printed results.

Here, we explore various methods to achieve this:

MIDJOURNEY'S BUILT-IN UPSCALER

Midjourney offers a "secondary diffusion" feature that essentially doubles the image resolution with each iteration. While convenient, this method comes with limitations.

While it increases the pixel count, it's important to understand that it **does not achieve true 300 dpi resolution**. Each upscaling step can introduce blur and distortion, especially in intricate designs. Additionally, repeated applications can lead to artifacts and a loss of detail. Therefore, relying solely on Midjourney's upscaler might **not be sufficient** for achieving professional-grade print quality.

EXTERNAL UPSCALING TOOLS

For more control and potentially better results, consider dedicated upscaling software. Several options are available, both free and paid:

- **FREE OPTIONS:**

  - **The Image Editor:** https://imageresizer.com/ This free online tool allows you to easily resize your image to your desired dimensions. However, it lacks advanced upscaling features and might not be suitable for complex artworks.

- GIMP: https://www.gimp.org/ This free and powerful open-source photo editor offers basic upscaling capabilities, along with other image manipulation tools. However, mastering GIMP requires some learning effort.

- **PAID OPTIONS:**

  - **Topaz Gigapixel AI:** https://www.topazlabs.com/ This advanced software utilizes AI technology to achieve impressive upscaling results while preserving details.

  - **Photoshop Super Resolution:** https://helpx.adobe.com/camera-raw/using/enhance.html Adobe Photoshop offers a dedicated "Super Resolution" feature for upscaling images. While not as powerful as dedicated AI-powered tools, it can deliver satisfactory results for simpler artworks.

FREE ALTERNATIVE: (MY GO-TO METHOD)

As a way to quickly and easily upscale my Midjourney images for personal or commercial printing projects, I often use a combination of two free online tools:

- **1. Resize and Download:**

  - Visit https://imageresizer.com/ and upload your Midjourney image.
  - Enter your desired final dimensions (e.g., inches or centimeters) and ensure the "Maintain aspect ratio" option is checked.
  - Download the resized image.

- **2. Convert DPI:**

  - Head to https://clideo.com/ and select the "DPI Converter" tool.
  - Upload your resized image and set the target DPI to 300 (you could set a bigger DPI if you need it)
  - Download the final, upscaled image. Job is done and ready to print!

Important Note: This free method might introduce **some quality loss** due to the limitations of basic resizing algorithms. However, it can be a quick and straightforward option for personal projects, especially when aiming for less intricate designs. So far, it has given me good results for generating large print images up to 90cm/35" .

Remember: Experiment with different upscaling methods and compare the results to find the approach that best suits your specific needs and desired print quality.

CONCLUSION:

By understanding these upscaling techniques, you can effectively bridge the gap between Midjourney's fixed resolution and the requirements of high-quality printing. Choose the method that best suits your needs and desired level of quality for your printed masterpiece.

FACTORS TO CONSIDER

PRINT SIZE:

The desired final size of your print (in inches or centimeters) guides the necessary upscaling level. Remember, aiming for 300 pixels per inch ensures high-quality results.

IMAGE COMPLEXITY:

Intricate designs with fine details require more aggressive upscaling compared to simpler artwork. Experiment with different methods to find the optimal balance between resolution and quality.

PRINTING SERVICE REQUIREMENTS:

Different printing services may have specific resolution recommendations based on the chosen material (t-shirts, canvas prints, etc.). Consulting your chosen service beforehand can prevent any surprises.

CMYK OR RGB:

For prints, it is generally recommended that colors are in CMYK and not RGB. Midjourney generates images in RGB, but most printing companies automatically convert the files to CMYK.

This can cause the colors to look slightly different, but it is usually not a problem. When converting from RGB to CMYK, some colors may not be able to be reproduced accurately. This is because the CMYK color space is smaller than the RGB color space.

However, most printing companies use sophisticated software to convert RGB files to CMYK. This software can usually reproduce the colors in your image very accurately.

- **Download PNG Format:** Opt for the PNG format when downloading your final artwork, as it preserves transparency and avoids compression artifacts, common in JPEGs.

- **Double-Check:** Before submitting your artwork for printing, meticulously scrutinize the upscaled image for potential issues like pixelation, blurring, or color banding.

By understanding these key points and employing the proper upscaling techniques, you can seamlessly transition your digital Midjourney creations into captivating physical prints. Now, go forth and transform your imagination into tangible masterpieces!

Now, let's get to the practical part with prompts-ready-to-use, which you can use as they are or you can complete/change them according to what you need.

We will put into practice everything we have seen previously, including all the necessary information to have the best images generated by the best prompts.

Now is the time to start playing!

2. Visualize Your Vision: Creating Mockups that Sell Your Designs

Want to turn your Midjourney creations into stunning mockups?

It's easier than you think, and the possibilities are endless!

In this section, we'll show you how to take your Midjourney images and transform them into realistic mockups that you can use to showcase your designs, impress your clients, and bring your creative visions to life.

Whether you're a seasoned designer or just starting out, we'll provide you with the step-by-step instructions and expert tips you need to create professional-quality mockups with ease.

So let's get started!

STEP BY STEP: EASY PEASY MOCKUPS

1 **Let's generate an image in Midjourney, like we always do.**

Prompt: a caterpillar logo , geometric shapes style, simple, icon style --no background --ar 1:1

Think ahead! The aspect ratio matters depending on what you're making.

2

The logo I got

Choose the image you want and press U + number in the order shown. In my case, I have chosen the first design: U1.

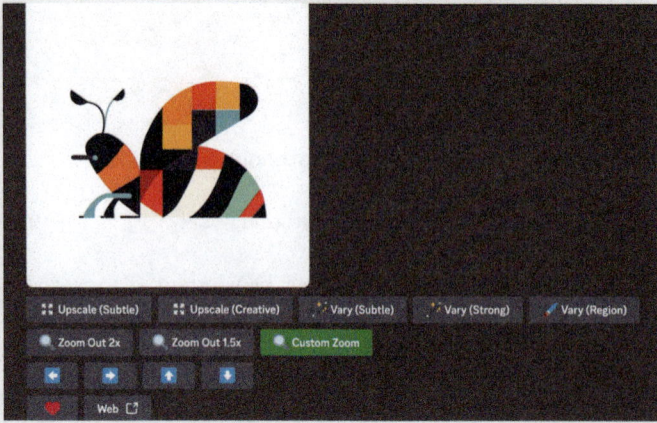

Click on **'custom Zoom'**.

A new window will open. Delete any existing text in the window and then write your prompt to generate the mockup. Here's the prompt I used:: ***product mockup, young woman wearing a white shirt --ar 5:7***

The final result!

CHECK OUT SOME MORE EXAMPLES BELOW

Prompt: *product mockup, poster hanging in a wall of a kitchen --ar 5:7*

Prompt: *product mockup, canva frame hanging in a wall of a children's room--ar 5:7*

Prompt: *product mockup, back of an iPhone case --ar 5:7*

So there you have it!

Remember, mockups are a powerful tool for designers. They can help you visualize your ideas, refine your designs, and impress your clients. Feel free to experiment and explore different mockup options!

8. PROMPTS TO SPARK YOUR MIDJOURNEY IMAGINATION

Introduction

Prompts to Spark Your Midjourney Imagination: Putting Theory into Practice

Now that you've explored the essential considerations for generating high-quality printed artwork from Midjourney, let's dive into the heart of the creative process - prompts! This section offers a curated list of prompts designed to ignite your artistic vision and equip you with practical examples of applying the information covered in this guide.

These prompts are crafted to embody the key strategies discussed earlier, including:

- Clear subject matter and style descriptions: Each prompt sets the foundation with specific details about the desired image's content and visual style.

- High-resolution considerations: While these prompts won't magically generate 300 dpi images, they lay the groundwork for successful upscaling by specifying preferred dimensions and encouraging awareness of resolution requirements.

- Customization potential: Every prompt is designed to be easily adapted. Feel free to modify any element – characters, styles, colors, and more – to tailor the prompt to your unique vision.

Remember, this is just the beginning! Treat these prompts as a springboard for your own creative exploration. Don't hesitate to experiment, modify, and combine elements to unlock your full Midjourney potential and bring your artistic ideas to life. Get ready to unleash your creativity! The following prompts are categorized into two sections:

- **Easier Prompts:** These are simpler prompts ideal for beginners or those wanting quick results.

- **More Complex Prompts:** These prompts offer greater detail and customization options for experienced users or those seeking more control over the generated image.

Despite all the information to make more specific prompts the choice is yours!

Midjourney can handle both short, open-ended prompts and detailed instructions. Short prompts encourage exploration and surprise, while detailed prompts give you more control over the final outcome.

1. Let's go! It's time to start using prompts!

Join Midjourney to create images from the discord channel:

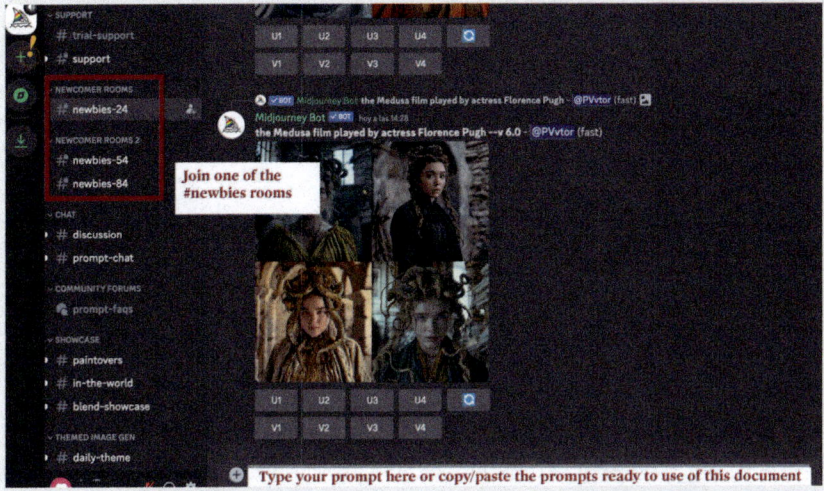

Ok! Now you are ready to start generating your own images!

2. EASIER PROMPTS: A SPARK FOR YOUR CREATIVITY

Easier prompts serve as a launchpad for your Midjourney exploration, offering a simple foundation to ignite your creative spark. They are designed with beginners and quick results in mind, focusing on clear and concise descriptions.

These prompts typically include:

- **A central subject:** This could be an object, person, animal, or scene.

- **Basic style or setting:** This might involve specifying a time period, artistic style, or general mood.

- **Limited details:** They avoid overwhelming complexity, allowing for easy customization and experimentation.

While "easier prompts" might not offer the same level of specific control as more intricate ones, they provide a solid starting point for:

- Learning the ropes of prompt crafting.
- Experimenting with different ideas and styles.
- Generating visually pleasing results quickly.

Think of them as stepping stones on your journey to mastering the art of Midjourney prompts. Feel free to adapt, modify, and combine these prompts to unlock your creative potential and craft truly unique Midjourney masterpieces.

IMPORTANT FOR ALL THE PROMPTS!

Don't forget: Start with the **/imagine** command before adding the prompt text

PROMPT 1. CAT

A **cyberpunk** cat **wearing a neon trench coat**, perched on a **rooftop** overlooking a futuristic **cityscape.**

You will get something like this:

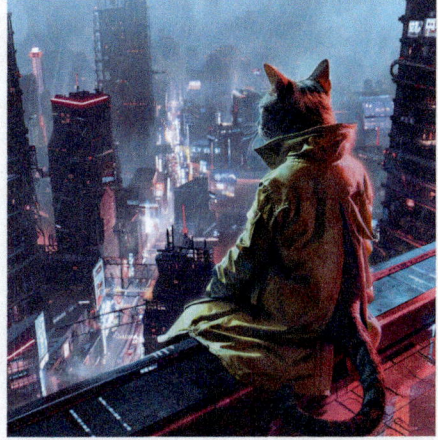

Expect similar results, but see what happens if you slightly change the prompt!

Prompt with some changes:

A **boho** cat wearing a **green** coat, perched on a rooftop overlooking a **mountain landscape.**

PROMPT 2. WATERFALL LANDSCAPE

A **watercolor painting** of a majestic waterfall cascading through a **lush green** forest.

You will get something like this:

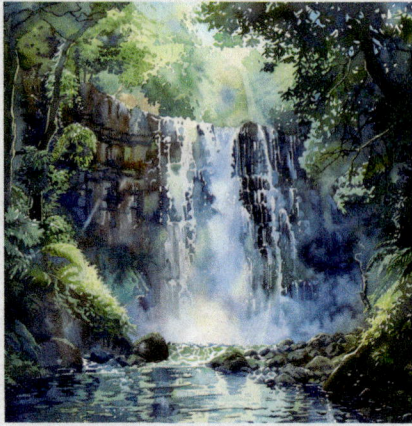

Expect similar results, but see what happens if you slightly change the prompt!

Prompt with some changes:

A **japanese art poster** of a majestic waterfall cascading through a **pastel color** forest.

PROMPT 3. ROCKET SHIP

A **retro-style** illustration of a rocket ship blasting off into a starry night sky. High resolution. Realistic.

You will get something like this:

Expect similar results, but see what happens if you slightly change the prompt!

Prompt with some changes:

A **art line style** illustration of a rocket ship blasting off into a **crescent moon casting a soft glow on a star-studded sky**. High resolution. Realistic.

PROMPT 4. MEDIEVAL SCENE

A **pixel art** scene of a bustling medieval marketplace filled with **colorful characters**. Realistic. High resolution

You will get something like this:

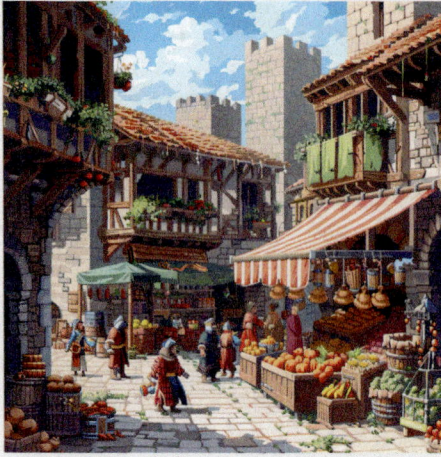

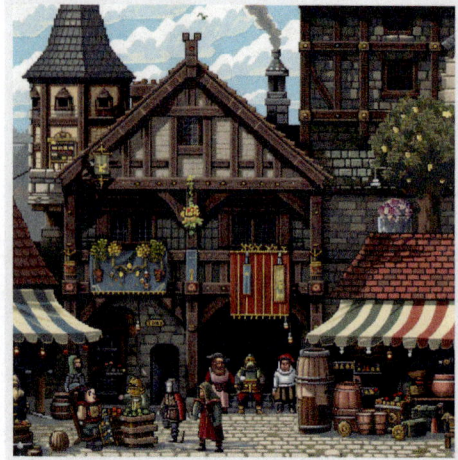

Expect similar results, but see what happens if you slightly change the prompt!

Prompt with some changes:

A **doodle style** scene of a bustling medieval marketplace. **Black and white**. Realistic. High resolution

PROMPT 5. UNICORN PORTRAIT

*A **pop art** portrait of a unicorn. Use **bold colors** and **thick** outlines. Rainbow colors background. High resolution and details.*

You will get something like this:

Expect similar results, but see what happens if you slightly change the prompt!

Prompt with some changes:

*A **detailed watercolour** portrait of a unicorn. Use **pastel colors** and **thin** outlines. Rainbow colors background. High resolution.*

PROMPT 6. LOGO

A **minimalist** logo for a cupcakes bakery shop. **Vibrant colors**. Use maximum 2 colors. No words. Transparent background

You will get something like this:

Expect similar results, but see what happens if you slightly change the prompt!

Prompt with some changes:

A **Kawaii** style logo for a cupcakes bakery shop. **Pink and purple** colors. Use maximum 2 colors. No words. Transparent background

A **cute cartoon** cat wearing an **astronaut helmet and holding a planet Earth globe**. Surround the cat with stars and a crescent moon. Keep the design simple and use **bold colors** suitable for printing on a t-shirt. Transparent background

You will get something like this:

Expect similar results, but see what happens if you slightly change the prompt!

Prompt with some changes:

A **vintage style** cat wearing an astronaut helmet and holding a planet Earth globe. Surround the cat with stars and a crescent moon. Keep the design simple and use **vibrant colors** suitable for printing on a t-shirt. Transparent background

PROMPT 8. INSTAGRAM TEMPLATE

An instagram template background. **Aesthetic style**. **Geometric shapes**. **Earth colors**. High resolution.

You will get something like this:

Expect similar results, but see what happens if you slightly change the prompt!

Prompt with some changes:

An instagram template background. **Minimalistic style. Flower and leaves. Black and white** colors. High resolution.

PROMPT 9. STICKER

*A **cute kawaii** sticker of a fluffy bunny holding a **heart-shaped balloon**. The bunny has big, sparkly eyes and blushing cheeks. Use **pastel colors** and a simple outline. Transparent background.*

You will get something like this:

Expect similar results, but see what happens if you slightly change the prompt!

Prompt with some changes:

*A **block print style** sticker of a fluffy bunny holding a heart-shaped balloon. The bunny has **small**, sparkly eyes and **gothic clothes**. **Black and white** colors and a simple outline. Transparent background.*

PROMPT 10. PATTERN

*A repeating pattern of different insects sketched in a **ballpoint pen style**. Include a variety of insects like butterflies, bees, ladybugs, and dragonflies. Use simple lines and **shading** to create a **textured look**.*

You will get something like this:

Expect similar results, but see what happens if you slightly change the prompt!

Prompt with some changes:

*A repeating pattern of different insects sketched in **geometric abstract style**. Include a variety of insects like butterflies, bees, ladybugs, and dragonflies. Use simple lines. **No shading**. **Vibrant colors**.*

3. MORE COMPLEX PROMPTS

Unveiling the Complexities: Crafting Masterful Midjourney Prompts

Welcome to the realm of complex prompts, where we delve deeper into the art of crafting prompts that unlock the full potential of Midjourney. Here, we transcend basic descriptions and delve into the details that breathe life into your imagined world. By incorporating a diverse range of elements, you'll transform your prompts from mere instructions into evocative narratives, capable of generating stunningly immersive and impactful Midjourney creations.

This section equips you with the tools to incorporate:

- **Descriptive language:** Vivid adjectives, adverbs, and similes bring your vision to life.
- **Sensory details:** Evoke sight, sound, smell, taste, and touch for a truly immersive experience.
- **Emotions:** Infuse your prompts with feelings like joy, sorrow, awe, or determination to set the emotional tone.
- **Action and movement:** Capture dynamism through verbs and descriptions of movement and posture.
- **Context and perspective:** Establish the setting, time period, and narrative viewpoint.

Beyond these essential elements, you can further enhance your prompts by:

- **Specifying artistic style and media:** Channel specific artistic styles like pointillism, surrealism, or watercolor painting.
- **Utilizing terms for detail and realism:** Employ terms like "highly detailed," "photorealistic," or "hyperrealistic" to achieve desired levels of detail.
- **Leveraging color theory terms:** Incorporate terms like "complementary colors," "analogous colors," or "warm/cool palette" to influence the color scheme.
- **Employing composition techniques:** Utilize terms like "rule of thirds," "leading lines," or "foreground/background" to guide the viewer's eye.
- **Describing lighting effects:** Specify lighting terms like "backlighting," "soft lighting," or "dramatic lighting" to create specific moods.

Additional Considerations:

- **Aspect ratio:** Define the desired image dimensions (e.g., square, rectangular, panoramic).
  You will define the aspect ratio at the end of your prompt adding: *--ar 5:4*

- **Negative prompts:** Excluding unwanted elements can further refine your results.

In a complex prompt, you can weave together a tapestry of even more elements beyond those covered here. Remember the details discussed throughout this guide, such as:

- **Camera angles:** Experiment with different camera angles, like a bird's-eye view for an expansive landscape or a close-up for an intimate portrait.

- **Focus and depth of field:** Specify where you want the viewer's focus to be and how much depth of field you desire.

- **Texture and material:** Describe the textures of objects and materials in your scene, like the roughness of weathered stone or the smoothness of flowing silk.

- **Weather and atmosphere:** Add details about the weather and atmosphere, such as a gentle breeze rustling leaves or a thick fog obscuring the background.

By incorporating these and other elements, you can create truly intricate and nuanced prompts that push the boundaries of Midjourney's capabilities and bring your artistic vision to life in stunning detail.

Ready to take your Midjourney skills to the next level? Let's dive into some complex prompt examples!

PROMPT 1. PATTERN

Watercolor painting, loose and expressive brushstrokes. Medium detail. A seamless repeating pattern suitable for clothing featuring vibrant tropical botanical elements like flowers, leaves, and fruits. Inspired by traditional Hawaiian tapa cloth patterns, with a modern twist in color and composition. The pattern should be organic and flowing, incorporating bold outlines and a sense of movement. Color palette: Vibrant and tropical colors, such as turquoise, fuchsia, orange, and emerald green. Use a repeating grid-based layout with the pattern seamlessly flowing across the image. No text, logos, or watermarks. --ar 1:1 --tile --v 5.2

Notes:

Using **--tile** that parameter generates images that can be used as repeating tiles to create seamless patterns for fabrics, wallpapers and textures.

--s 100 parameter influences how strongly this training is applied. Low stylization values produce images that closely match the prompt but are less artistic. High stylization values create images that are very artistic but less connected to the prompt.

Now, look what **--tile** parameter accomplished. I'm going to put the same image 4 times to show you how the pattern fits together perfectly. This will allow you to create large pattern images that can be used for printing fabrics, among other things.

PROMPT 2. WALL ART POP ART STYLE

Pop art style, high detail. A vibrant portrait of a mischievous cat wearing a pair of oversized sunglasses, tongue sticking out playfully. The cat is adorned with a crown made of colorful candies and surrounded by a swirling background of pop art elements like speech bubbles, stars, and polka dots. Use a bold and contrasting color palette, incorporating warm and cool tones for a dynamic feel. No text, logos, or watermarks. --ar 2:3 --style raw --s 100 --q1 --v 5.2

Notes:

--style raw uses an alternative model that may work well for users already comfortable with prompting who want more control over their images. Images made with --style raw have less automatic beautification applied, which can result in a more accurate match when prompting for specific styles.

The parameter **--q1** is used to control the quality of the generated image. It takes a value between 0.25 and 1

PROMPT 3. WALL ART ABSTRACT

Abstract expressionist style, high detail. A vibrant and chaotic landscape, capturing the energy and movement of nature. Bold brushstrokes in contrasting colors like crimson, ochre, and turquoise create swirling clouds, textured mountains, and a rushing river. Use impasto techniques for added texture and dimension. Imagine this scene viewed from a bird's-eye perspective, showcasing the vastness and grandeur of the natural world. No text, logos, or watermarks. --ar 3:2 --s 100 --q 1 --w 250 --v 5.2

Notes:

--**weird** or --**w** parameter. This parameter introduces quirky and offbeat qualities to your generated images, resulting in unique and unexpected outcomes.

--weird accepts values: 0–3000

PROMPT 4. PRINTING FOR A SHIRT

Watercolor painting, medium detail. A bohemian-inspired design, centered on a weathered cream background. A crescent moon , rendered in soft silver and gold hues. Accentuate the design with small watercolor splatters in contrasting colors like burnt orange and teal for a playful boho touch. Utilize negative space effectively for a balanced and breathable composition. No text, logos, or watermarks. --ar 1:1 --s 100 --q 1 --v 5.2

PROMPT 5. WALL ART / PRINTING

Grafitti paint, medium detail. A streetwear-inspired design. A kiwi bird at the center. In vibrant colours. Underground grunge style design. No text, logos, or watermarks. --ar 1:1 --s 100 --q 1 --v 5.2

You don't need very long prompts to get unique images.

PROMPT 7. INSTAGRAM TEMPLATE

Instagram template. Minimalist japanese style. Pastel colors --no words --ar 9:16

PROMPT 8. ILLUSTRATED CARD

Illustrated card, Watercolor, complementary colors, cuteness, illustration, hand-drawn illustrations, a drawing of a young girl and tree, in the style of yuumei, happiness, minimalism --no watermark --chaos 5 --ar 9:16 --style raw --stylize 750

PROMPT 9. 3D

Close up of cute hipster women 3D cartoon character, riding a skateboard, 3D rendering illustration, minimalistic, soft studio lighting, solid color background --ar 3:2 --s 100 --q 1 --v 5.2

PROMPT 10. INVITATION CARD

For an elegant spring invitation, design a collection of romantic watercolor flower clipart on a white background that minimally borders the content. Begin with a small cluster of delicate cherry blossoms and graceful tulips as individual clipart pieces, one in each corner of the invitation, forming a 90-degree angle, accented by strands of fine baby's breath. These pieces should be designed to allow for a striking and dynamic arrangement that stretches towards the upper right corner, ensuring the floral clipart adds a bold and energetic touch to the invitation's design. --ar 9:16 --no mockup --s 100 --q 1 --v 5.2

Notes:

Use negative prompt as **--no mockup** in this example.

PROMPT 11. POSTER ILLUSTRATION

No words, vintage poster illustration, a vintage eyewear ads for sunglasses female monkey with a smile 1940s, in the style of 1970– present, hyperrealism, orange and brown, oil portraitures, socially minded. --ar 2:3 --v 5.2

PROMPT 12. LIFESTYLE

Realistic photo of a happy mum, sitting in a chair, helping her young kid with her sport shoes, in the dresser room of their Montessori school, detailed, playful emote. High resolution. Closed up. Hyperrealistic --ar 3:4 --stylize 50 --v 5.2

PROMPT 13. LOGO

Logo with plain solid colors caterpillar. no words. simple lines. Black outline. Transparent Background. No watermark. --ar 1:1 --stylize 250 --v 5.2

You've Arrived: The Gateway to Infinite Creativity with Midjourney

Congratulations! You've reached the final chapter, unlocking a universe of creative potential with Midjourney. The knowledge and skills you've gained empower you to transform ideas into stunning visuals, regardless of experience.

This journey began empowering beginners, but you've become a seasoned Midjourney user. Now, confidently apply your newfound abilities to any project – marketing campaigns, personal art, or anything your imagination conjures.

Remember, the possibilities within Midjourney are as vast as your creativity. Keep exploring to discover even more advanced techniques and elevate your creations to new heights!

The Wellspring of Support

Should you encounter questions along your artistic path, never hesitate to reach out. I'm here to guide you as you unlock the full potential of Midjourney.

Share the Spark of Creativity

Midjourney transcends being just a tool; it's a vibrant community brimming with artistic minds. Leaving a review for this guide would be a fantastic way to empower others and help them embark on their creative journeys with Midjourney. Additionally, by sharing your newfound skills, you can inspire others to explore the boundless possibilities this platform offers.

The Dawn of AI-Powered Creativity

Artificial intelligence, particularly tools like Midjourney, presents a future brimming with creative potential. In the near future, AI-powered tools like this one will likely become commonplace. By learning Midjourney now, you'll be a pioneer in this exciting new artistic landscape.

The Canvas Awaits

The world of Midjourney beckons. Grab your imagination, unleash your creativity, and prepare to be amazed by the boundless possibilities that await!

Contact me!

Gèni Serra

dit.and.fem@gmail.com

ditandfem

etsy.com/shop/DitAndFem/

Printed in Dunstable, United Kingdom

HAVE A
FUNJOURNEY!

ISBN 9798884441156

9 798884 441156

90000